THE
OXYRHYNCHUS PAPYRI
VOLUME XXXVII

THE
OXYRHYNCHUS PAPYRI

VOLUME XXXVII

EDITED WITH NOTES

BY

E. LOBEL, M.A.

Graeco-Roman Memoirs, No. 53

———

PUBLISHED FOR

THE BRITISH ACADEMY

BY THE

EGYPT EXPLORATION SOCIETY

2–3 DOUGHTY MEWS, LONDON W.C.I

1971

PRINTED IN GREAT BRITAIN
AT THE UNIVERSITY PRESS, OXFORD, BY VIVIAN RIDLER
PRINTER TO THE UNIVERSITY
AND PUBLISHED FOR
THE BRITISH ACADEMY
BY THE EGYPT EXPLORATION SOCIETY
2–3 DOUGHTY MEWS, LONDON W.C. I

ALSO SOLD BY
BERNARD QUARITCH, 5–8 LOWER JOHN STREET, GOLDEN SQUARE, WIV 6AB
KEGAN PAUL, TRENCH, TRUBNER & CO., 43 GREAT RUSSELL STREET, W.C. I

PREFACE

FRAGMENTS of twenty-three papyrus manuscripts have been assembled in this part, transcribed and annotated entirely by Mr. E. Lobel. They include small scraps of lyric verse, lines from tragedy and from old comedy (as well as commentaries on both these genres, which are rich in quotations), hexameter verses, a piece of a prose history of Egypt (published for the light its wording throws on a passage in Aeschylus), and a fragment of a pedigree of Theoxena, daughter of Agathocles.

Thanks are due to the Oxford University printer for the care taken over a difficult piece of type-setting, and to his staff for willing help in preparing photographs as a basis for the collotype reproduction done by the Cotswold Press. Mr. Richard Carden made the index.

P. J. PARSONS
J. R. REA
E. G. TURNER
General Editors of the
Graeco-Roman Memoirs

January 1970

CONTENTS

TEXTS

TABLE OF PAPYRI

* Dates are A.D. unless the contrary is specifically stated

LIST OF PLATES

NUMBERS AND PLATES

NOTE ON THE METHOD OF PUBLICATION

THE method of publication follows that adopted in Part XXXV. As there, the dots indicating letters unread and, within square brackets, the estimated number of lost letters are printed slightly below the line. Corrections and annotations which appear to be in a different hand from that of the original scribe are printed in thick type. Square brackets [ ] indicate a lacuna, round brackets ( ) the resolution of a symbol or abbreviation, angular brackets ⟨ ⟩ a mistaken omission in the original, braces { } a superfluous letter or letters, double square brackets ⟦ ⟧ a deletion, the signs ' ' an insertion above the line. Dots within brackets represent the estimated number of letters lost or deleted, dots outside brackets mutilated or otherwise illegible letters. Dots under letters indicate that the reading is doubtful. Letters not read or marked as doubtful in the literal transcript may be read or appear without the dot marking doubt in the reconstruction, if the context justifies this. Lastly, heavy Arabic numerals refer to Oxyrhynchus papyri printed in this and preceding volumes, ordinary numerals to lines, small Roman numerals to columns.

NEW CLASSICAL FRAGMENTS

2801. Lyric (Alcman ?)

A scrap of no present value, but consistent as far as it goes with attribution to Alcman.

The writing is a good-sized upright bookhand, comparable with **1084**, to be dated in the earlier part of the second century. The lection signs appear to be due to a different pen.

```
             ·     ].[      ·
        ]..[   ]..[
        ]επακουϲομε[
          ·]ἄλοϲοιατ’α[]...[
  5     ] υμνιομεϲᾱπίαιϲ[
        ].πον[[ο]]ϲευρ[ ]...[
             ·     ·      ·
```

Ll. 1 seq. largely stripped   3 Of ε[only the left-hand arc   4 ·], above the line the top of a loop   ]...[, on a narrow projection the tops of letters, of which bases on a single fibre below; e.g. ρ followed by a circle, and this by a dot level with their tops   5 Below α ink representing a letter or sign relating to the following line   6]., the lower part of a stroke curving down from left; e.g. μ   Of π only the feet   Above the cancelled o the surface is destroyed   ]...[, scattered specks

4 The ink above the line before ἄλοϲ is consistent with θ and I have therefore considered the possibility that ϲάλοϲ, clarified as θάλοϲ, is to be recognized. But prima facie θ is too far to the left by a letter to admit of this account, though ϲάλοϲ may all the same be true. ἐν ϲάλεϲϲι, Alcm. 15.

οἵά τε 'as', Alcm. 56, 4.

5 ὑμνίομεϲ ὑμνιοιϲᾶν Alcm. 3 fr. 1, 5. For -ίομεϲ (however to be spelt or scanned) cf. e.g. Aristoph. *Lysistr.* 1002, 1148.

ἀπίαιϲ ἀπιομ[ήδ]ει Pind. *Pae.* vii 7, but ἠπιόφρον Bacchyl. xiii 78. Doubtful at **2624** fr. 28, 5; ἠ- in quotation, Stesich. 223, 2 PMG.

6 The cancelled o represents an indispensable vowel, which must have been written above, where the surface is destroyed.

2802. On Alcman ?

The mention of Alcman, whose name is to be recognized in two places (ll. 5, 17), and the prima facie acceptability of the hypothesis that his date is one of the subjects treated, make it reasonable to see in this scrap remains of a life of or a commentary on this poet, but too much is lost for any coherent information to be extracted from it. I see no trace of what is a favourite topic in other places where his life is discussed, whether he was a Lydian or a Spartan, though someone's πατρίϲ is mentioned at l. 13.

The text is written on the back of a piece of papyrus of which **2821** occupies the front, in a small loose hand with a few cursive forms and simple suspensions. I suppose it may be dated in the latter part of the second century.

$$
\begin{array}{cl}
 & \cdot \qquad \cdot \qquad \cdot \\
 &]\ldots[\\
 &]\eta\rho\omega\,.[\\
 &]\,.\,\upsilon\,.\,\phi\lambda\eta\nu\alpha\phi\,.\,.[\\
 &]\nu o\varsigma\epsilon\nu\bar{\gamma}\ \overset{}{\pi}\epsilon[\\
5 &]\tau\iota\ \bar{\beta}\alpha\lambda\kappa\mu\alpha[\\
 &]\,.\,.\,\upsilon\tau\epsilon\rho o\upsilon\pi\epsilon\rho[\\
 &]\,.\,\tau\epsilon\rho o\varsigma\ o\delta'\nu[\\
 &]\nu\eta\rho\omega\alpha\upsilon[\\
 &]\,.\,\upsilon\mu\overset{}{\pi}\rho\epsilon\varsigma[\\
10 &]\,.\,\rho\tau\omega\,.\,\rho\alpha\kappa\,.[\\
 &]\,.\,\kappa\rho o\nu\alpha\pi\omega[\\
 &]\lambda o\upsilon\mu\epsilon\nu o\upsilon[\\
 &]\nu\pi\alpha\tau\rho\iota\delta o\varsigma\alpha\upsilon\tau o\upsilon[\\
 &]\,.\,\nu\kappa\alpha\theta o\upsilon\varsigma\epsilon\gamma\epsilon\nu\epsilon\,[\\
15 &]\pi\alpha\iota\delta\epsilon\iota\alpha\varsigma\delta'\phi^{?}\alpha\rho\eta\,[\\
 &]\tau\iota\kappa\eta\nu\ddot{\iota}\varsigma\tau o\rho\iota\alpha\varsigma\,[\\
 &]\mu\alpha\nu\omega\varsigma\tau\epsilon\mu o\upsilon\,[\\
 &]\rho o\alpha\upsilon\tau o\upsilon\pi o\lambda\upsilon\gamma\epsilon\,[\\
 &]\tau\epsilon\rho o\varsigma\delta'\tau'\overset{\mu\epsilon\tau}{[\![\pi\rho\,.]\!]}\,.\,.[\\
20 &]\alpha\xi\alpha\pi\alpha\nu\tau'\mu\epsilon\tau\rho\alpha[\\
 &]\epsilon\pi o\iota\eta\varsigma\epsilon\nu\,.\,[\,.\,.\,]\,.\,.[\\
 &]\rho\tau\,.\,\epsilon\dot{\tau}\psi\upsilon\ldots\rho[\\
 &]\,.\,[\,]\,.\,[\,]\,.\,.\,[\,]\ldots[\\
 &]\epsilon\iota\nu\alpha[\,]\,.\,[\\
25 &]o\mu o\,[\\
 &]\tau\ldots[\\
 &]\,.\,\varsigma\epsilon\chi[\\
 &]\alpha\varsigma\rho\epsilon[\\
 &]\dot{\tau}\,.[\\
 & \cdot \qquad \cdot \qquad \cdot
\end{array}
$$

1 A stroke starting below the line and rising to right, followed by a horizontal stroke on the line, then a horizontal stroke at mid letter touching the upper end of a stroke hooked strongly to right at its foot, followed by the foot of an upright; perhaps four letters　　2 .[, the lower part of an upright hooked to right　　3]., the right-hand ends of strokes touching the top of the left-hand branch and the bottom of the foot of v　From the top of the right-hand branch of v a stroke (ligature?) descends slightly to the top of a slightly convex upright　　..[, what now looks like c followed by an upright 6]., a speck at mid letter, followed by a sign I cannot interpret, most like the left-hand stroke of an unfinished β or a ξ with no central zigzag　　7]., the upper half of η? Not prima facie $a\iota$　　9]., specks slightly below the level of the top of the letters　　10]., the right-hand end of a cross-stroke, as of γ, having above it the right-hand end of a horizontal stroke　If ρ, the loop not closed　Of ω only the left-hand half, but I prefer to ϱ[.]　Before ρ ϵ appears likeliest, though anomalous; δ hardly admissible　.[, the left-hand arc of a small circle　　11]., the upper part of an upright with ink to right of its top; perhaps]$\epsilon\iota$ should be written　　13 Above the left-hand side of]ν elements of a stroke curving down to left. See comm.　　14]., the upper end of a stroke curving down to left 19 ..[, a speck on the line having above and to right the upper end of a stroke descending to right, perhaps a, followed by the top of a loop, level with the top of the letters, having below it on the line the start of a stroke rising to right　　20 Of a[only the loop, but I think not o　　22 Of]ρ only the tail　Between τ and ϵ an upright having on its tip an angular sign like the upper parts of a small ζ and apparently descending into l. 23　Of v only the upper part of the left-hand arm　After v the lower part of an upright, the foot of an upright, a speck on the line　Before ρ[perhaps a represented by its tail　　23]....[, $\rho\mu$ look acceptable for the second and third letters, though this does not account for a dot above ρ, which suggests ϕ but I am not sure is ink. ρ might be preceded by v, represented by the start of the fork. After μ a dot level with the top of the letters　　24 Of]ϵ only the ligature　].[, the lower part of an upright descending below the line　　26 ....[, scribbled; the last two letters might be $a\iota$, the others suggest some combination of κ, μ, ω　　27]., a slightly concave upright with faint traces to left; perhaps].ι should be written　　29 Of]τ only the left-hand end of the cross-stroke.

3 $\phi\lambda\eta\nu\alpha\phi$.. The ink is incompatible with any form of $\phi\lambda\eta\nu\alpha\phi\acute{\alpha}\omega$ or any case of $\phi\lambda\acute{\eta}\nu\alpha\phi\sigma\varsigma$. $\phi\lambda\eta\nu\alpha$-$\phi\epsilon\acute{\iota}$[$\alpha$, for $\phi\lambda\eta\nu\alpha\phi\acute{\iota}\alpha$, itself not strongly attested, may be acceptable.

4]$\nu\sigma\varsigma$ $\grave{\epsilon}\nu$ ($\tau\rho\acute{\iota}\tau\omega\iota$) $\pi(\epsilon\rho\grave{\iota})$ ϵ['-nus in Bk. iii *On* —'.

5 Perhaps ($\delta\epsilon\acute{\upsilon}\tau\epsilon\rho\sigma\varsigma$) $Ἀλκμά$[ν, implying a catalogue. $Ἀλκ$]$μάν$ again at l. 17.

6 seq. Apparently comparatives and therefore -$\sigma\nu$ μ($\grave{\epsilon}\nu$) $\pi\rho\epsilon\varsigma$[$\beta\upsilon\tau\epsilon\rho$- in l. 9 is a reasonable shot.

11 μ]{ϵ}$\iota\kappa\rho\acute{\sigma}\nu$?

13 Though]ν is slightly anomalous, I do not think].$a\iota$ is a likely combination of the ink described.

14 seq. Perhaps $\chi\rho\acute{\sigma}\nu$]$\omega\nu$ $\kappa\alpha\theta$' $\sigma\grave{\upsilon}\varsigma$ $\grave{\epsilon}\gamma\acute{\epsilon}\nu\epsilon$|$\tau\sigma$ 'of his times'.

After $\delta(\epsilon)$ $\phi\eta(\varsigma\iota\nu)$ one might expect a proper name. I can suggest nothing suitable in *Are*-.

17 seqq. π]$\rho\grave{\sigma}$ $\alpha\grave{\upsilon}\tau\sigma\hat{\upsilon}$ $\pi\sigma\lambda\grave{\upsilon}$ $\gamma\epsilon$|ν- 'much earlier than him in date'. In relation to Alcman this might be said of $Mσυ$|$\varsigma\alpha\hat{\iota}σς$, but I do not believe that the choice of this legendary figure as a point of reference is likely.

19 seq. $\grave{\alpha}\pi$]$\alpha\xi\alpha\pi\alpha\nu$- seems unavoidable but τ' as equivalent to $\tau\eta\varsigma$ is incompatible with it. But neither is it prima facie detachable. Although I can find no other extension of τ' but $\tau\eta\varsigma$, ν' is *vac* at P. Berol. 9780 (Didymus) xiii 28 and ρ' is $\rho\alpha\varsigma$ in the same papyrus.

2803. STESICHORUS?

The fragment which I have placed first of the following scraps of a roll preserves on its front remains representing two columns, the second shown by the stichometrical letter in its margin to have contained the hundredth verse of the roll, the first consequently to have stood at or near its beginning. On the back of this first column are the first letters of a two-lined entry running in the same direction as the text, which must when complete have extended still further towards the beginning of the roll. There can be no question that it was intended to indicate the contents. Another example of this method may be seen in **2741** Commentary on Eupolis *Μαρικᾶς*; an alternative, namely, writing the contents at right angles to the text inside, in **2538** Alcaeus, Book i (or iv).

For *Cτη*[I do not think it possible to find any completion but *Cτησιχόρου*. So far as I can judge from the defective evidence the style of the text, though not distinctly confirmatory, is not inconsistent with this ascription, and if the piece was, as appears, the subject of comment by Theon and Aristonicus, the author is likely to have been a major figure. The only ground for questioning 'Stesichorus' is *ιππ*[in the second line. More than a dozen names of pieces by or attributed to him are recorded; none beginning so and none, so far as I see, of which *ιππ*- might begin an alternative title. But as there were twenty-six books of his poems (Suid. in v.) it would not be surprising, if a hitherto unattested poem emerged. Of the subject of this piece I see nothing to say except that in part at least it may have been 'matter of Troy'.

The text is written in a bookhand of a not very common type which I suppose might well fall into the first century B.C. The copyist himself seems to have added most or all of the accents (none 'Doric'), breathings, and 'longs' or 'shorts'. At least three, and perhaps more, pens seem to be recognizable in the marginalia added, as far as I can tell, in the late first or second century. The names of Aristonicus and Theon provide for some a rough *terminus post quem*.

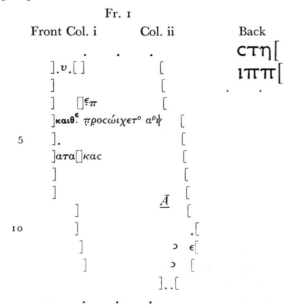

Fr. 1

Fr. 1 Front col. i 1]., perhaps the right-hand end of the cross-stroke and the right-hand end of the base of ε   .[, an upright   4 *marg.* Below ε of θε a dot (not ε doubtful)   Of π only the left-hand upright and the extreme right-hand end of the cross-stroke; of ρ only the back of the loop and the extreme lower end of the tail   5]. perhaps the right-hand side of α; slightly anomalous, but not λ   6 If any letter is lost between α and κ, the only possibility seems to be ι

Col. ii 10 .[, on the line a loop open to right, above it a short piece of an upright; perhaps parts of letters in different lines

At the bottom, to left of the column a large blot from the right-hand side of which there emerge parts of two letters

Fr. 1 Col. i 3 *marg.* No doubt θεπ as at fr. 4, 1 *marg.*

4 *marg.* καὶ Θέ(ων)?, again at fr. 4, 4 *marg.*

προcοίχεcθαι hitherto only Pind. *Pyth.* vi 4. In Stesichorus ποτώιχετο would be expected.

AᵖNᶥ not certainly resolved. For the reasons given at **2387** fr. 1 *mg. 4* I believe that Ἀριcτόνικοc is the likeliest extension.

Col. ii 8–9 *marg.* Ā̄ 'Line 100' on right.

11 seq. The *antisigma* as in the Stesichorus manuscript **2617** fr. 13 (*a*) 14, fr. 19 ii 7, fr. 46 ii 6. I cannot see any relation between the two here and the two in the margin of fr. 7, 6.

Fr. 2

5

Fr. 2 1]., on the line the end of a stroke from left   Of ο only the lower part   ...[, the foot of an upright, the start of a stroke rising to right, the start of a slightly convex stroke rising to right, perhaps α   5 .[, an apex, λ suggested

Fr. 3   Fr. 4

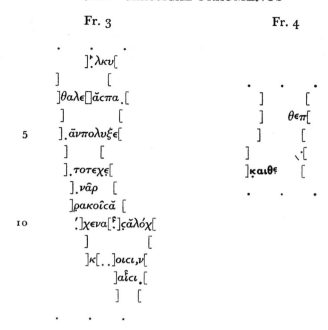

Fr. 3 1]., the lower part of a slightly convex upright; η and ε]ι both anomalous   3 .[, prima facie the left-hand side of η, but perhaps a damaged ρ   5]., the right-hand arc of a circle; ρ suggested by its position   7]., the upper part of an upright   8]., an upright   10 Of ς only the top right-hand curve   Above χ a speck, presumably belonging to a marginal note   13 .[, the foot of an upright

Fr. 4 I believe I can identify fibres running across from fr. 3 which fix the level of this fragment as shown

3 ·[, what resembles the upper left-hand part of a small τ, slightly tilted to right and having a thin stroke descending to right from the end of the cross-stroke; I cannot tell whether letter or sign

Fr. 3 3 I suppose -θᾰλέας (as, e.g., Pind. *Pae.* vi 181 εὐ-, Bacchyl. xiii 69, 229 παν-, not -θᾱλ- as e.g. Pind. *Pyth.* ix 72 εὐ-, *Nem.* ix 48 νεο-).

5 If Polyxena, as daughter of Priam consonant with the mention of other Trojan matter in frr. 5; 11. (Her slaughter by Neoptolemus mentioned by Ibycus, PMG **304**.)

8 seq. ἀρ|ξε or the like implied.

9 δ]ρακοῖσα. δρακών and cases not frequently seen; Pindar, who has several instances of the participle, always uses δρακείς, peculiar to himself.

10 There seems no alternative to αἶς. If ἀλόχοις follows, Priam might well be referred to.

Fr. 4 1 θεπ at fr. 1 i 3 *marg.* stands about half way between the columns. θε may be Θέων here (and in other marginal notes in different writing), but I cannot guess what he is cited for, which may or may not depend on the interpretation of π.

4 καὶ Θέ(ων) as at fr. 1 i 4 *marg.* I do not know whether the dot under ε is meant to differentiate this θ from the other.

Fr. 5

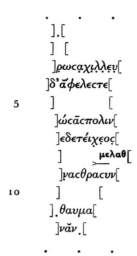

].[
] [
]ρωϲαχιλλευ[
]δ᾿ἄφελεϲτε[
5   ]   [
]ωϲᾱϲπολιν[
]εδετέιχεοϲ[
]   μελαθ[
]ϝαϲθραϲυν[
10   ]   [
].θαυμα[
]ϝᾰν.[

Fr. 5 3 Of ι only the extreme lower end, of υ only the foot   7 Of ϲ[only a trace of the left-hand arc   11]., on a single fibre perhaps parts of the bottom right-hand angle of ν   12 .[, the top left-hand arc of a circle

Fr. 5 3 If ἥρωϲ Ἀχιλλεύϲ, cf., e.g., Pind. *Pyth.* xi 31 ἥρωϲ Ἀτρεΐδαϲ, *Pae.* vii 13 ἥρωα Τήνερον. In the reverse order perhaps at **2618** fr. 1 i 3 (Stesichorus?), cf., e.g., Pind. *Pyth.* viii 51.

4 Accented to preclude ἀφελέϲ or ἀφελεϲτε[ρ-? ἄφελεϲ remains ambiguous: ἄφελε imperative, ἄφελε (v. Chandler, *Accent.* § 816) for ἀφεῖλε, ἄφελεϲ for ἀφεῖλεϲ.

6 -]ωϲαϲ aorist participle. In Stesichorus -ϲαιϲ would be expected.[1] But errors are found; contrast in the analogous case (α)παϲιν **2619** fr. 1 i 13 with ἀπαιϲ[- **2619** fr. 16, 16 (Stesichorus?).

[I now think it very likely that I should have recognized]ωϲαϲπολ[.]ν at **2619** fr. 28, 1.]

In the context perhaps a word meaning 'destroy' (and in l. 9 a word meaning 'kill') suits.

[1] In fact the only relevant parallel I have found in Stesichorus is in **185** PMG, περάϲαϲ, but that is a quotation and not good evidence for dialectal forms of the παράδοϲιϲ. For what it is worth the παράδοϲιϲ of Simonides offers τελέϲϲαιϲ at **2430** fr. 90 i 3.

Fr. 6   Fr. 7

```
          ]κα[                              ].[
          ]ϲ.[].[                           ]...[
          ].ϲ.ντριϲ [              ]...[ ] οτε       [
          ]..ἐβᾰνοπλ[              ]ώμενοϲ           [
    5     ]. οιϲ..εϲ/ωγ[      5    ]ουδέ ὸτο         [
          .ππ[]..ϲ.[               ]οοβριμ[ ].
          ]..ναριϲτ[              ]οτοξοτ.[ ]..      [
          ]..δα [                  ]επᾰϲϲυτεροι    :[
          ].[]...[                 ]                [
          ].[                      ]..δ[].χᾱ.ιν     [
                                   ]                [
```

Frr. 6 and **7** have a good many points of resemblance, front and back, but I cannot follow any fibres down from one into the other. Both are rubbed

Fr. 6 2 .[, the upper left-hand arc of a circle   3]., a dot on the line   Between ϲ and ν specks perhaps representing the ends of the overhang and cross-stroke of ε   4].., prima facie the lower part of the right-hand half of ω with ἀπόϲτροφοϲ, followed at an interval by the lower part of ε or ϲ   ἐ all trace of the cross-stroke has vanished   λ[, I am not sure that α can be ruled out 5 *marg. 1* To left of the letters two traces   Of ρ only the upper half   Between ϲ and ε the top of a loop, followed by a small c-shaped stroke   *2* At an interval to left of π the lower part of a stroke, descending from left, with a dot below its upper end and a dot to right level with its upper end ; ⊼ one possibility   Before ϲ two dots on the line and a dot, perhaps ligatured to ϲ, level with the top of the letters   After ϲ a cross-stroke level with the top of the letters   6].., a dot on the line, followed by a dot on the line with a speck vertically above it; ι not suggested   Over τ a thick dot, perhaps casual ink   7 Before δ faint dispersed traces. Immediately before δ perhaps the back of the loop of ρ   8]...[, I think part of a marginal note

Fr. 7 1 seq. Faint traces; l. 2 apparently part of a marginal note   3]...[, specks on the line 5 After ἐ the lower part of a stroke curving down from left; ϲ not suggested   6 *marg. 2* the left-hand arc of a circle; not much like the loop of α   7 *marg.* with a thick point, which I do not see elsewhere, the beginnings of two lines in which I cannot recognize letters   9].., the lower part of a stroke descending from left, having above it the right-hand end of a cross-stroke, followed by the lower part of an upright; perhaps]ᾱι   After δ[] specks   After ά faint elements of an upright

Fr. 6 5 *marg. 1* The first word could be verified, if correctly deciphered. / presumably (ἐϲτιν). *2* There is a space between the traces before ππ and those letters. I do not see how to avoid supposing that there is a mistake.

6 I think that just possibly]ον or]ων may be elicited.

Fr. 7 5 seq. το|ξοτ-?

6 *marg.* The *antisigma* is said to be prefixed to verses which for one reason or another are unsuitable where they stand. This use does not seem applicable to marginal additions.

9 χάριν hardly avoidable.

Fr. 8   Fr. 9

```
      ·      ·       ·                          ·      ·
      ]    [                                  ]δα[
  ].αν· γ[                                      ]  [
      ].[                                      ]τρ[
   ·        ·        ·                      ·      ·      ·
```

Fr. 8 1]., a dot level with the top of the letters 2 A horizontal stroke touching the bottom of the upper part of a vertical stroke; η not suggested

Fr. 10

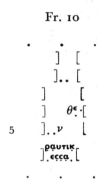

```
          ·      ·      ·
          ]    [
          ].. [
          ]        [
          ]     θε ·[
   5      ]..ν     [
        ]ρ̣α̣υτικ[
        ].εϲϲα.[
             ·        ·
```

Fr. 10 2].., on the line a dot with the right-hand end of a cross-stroke above, followed by a short upright with a speck to left of its top 4 To right of θε two faded parallel strokes near the line; below them what looks like a flattened λ but is perhaps an anomalous διπλῆ ὠβελιϲμένη 5].., two specks just below the level of the top of the letters, between them the upper part of an upright 6 *marg.* 2]., the upper part of a slightly concave upright .[, a speck on the line and a dot below

Fr. 10 6 There is now no sign of ink before ρ, and I may have misinterpreted *antisigma*.

Fr. 11

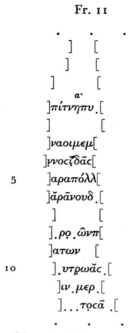

```
          ·              ·
        ]    [
        ]    [
        ]        [
           ἀ·
      ]πίτνηπυ.[
        ]        [
      ]ναοιμεμ[
      ]ννος̣δᾱς[
5    ]αραπόλλ[
      ]ἄρᾱνουδ.[
        ]        [
      ].ρο̣.ῶνπ[
      ]ατων    [
10   ].υτρωᾱς.[
      ]ιν.μερ.[
      ]...το̣σᾱ.[
          ·              ·
```

Fr. 11 1 .[, an upright   4 Of]ν only the lower part of the second upright   6 .[, the lower part of a stroke rising to right; α not particularly suggested   8]., about mid letter the base of a small circle   Between ρ and ω̂ a dot on the line; the spacing suggests γ or π   10]., the right-hand arc of a circle   Of ρ only the upper part of the loop   .[, an upright   11 Between ν and μ the lower part of a slightly forward-sloping stroke, nearer to ν   .[, perhaps elements of a circle, but I am not sure how much is ink   12]..., specks level with the top of the letters on either side of the top of a circle   .[, prima facie υ but inordinately short-stalked and having a long serif to left   There appears to be a short stroke above the line between the last two letters

Fr. 11 1 πίτνα imperfect of πίτνημι, after *Il.* xxi 7.
3 Δα]ναοί?
4 Ἐ]ννοσίδας hitherto only Pindaric.

Fr. 12

```
        ·      ·      ·
      ].νε[
      ]    [
      ]ιν  [
        ·      ·      ·
```

Fr. 13

```
          ·      ·      ·
        ].[
        ].α[
        ]η[
        ]δω[
```

Fr. 12 1]., the lower part of a stroke descending from left, α or λ

Fr. 13 1 The foot of an upright   2]., the lower part of a stroke descending from left

Fr. 14　　　　　　　　　　　　　Fr. 15

```
  ].·.[                              ].·.[
  ].co[                              ]oc[
  ]ac.[                              ]επ[
  ].ρᾰ.[
5  ].[
```

Fr. 14 2]. an upright　　3 .[, an upright
4]., the right-hand parts of η̄ suggested　.[, a
dot not quite level with the top of the letters
5].[, a cross-stroke, too near l. 4 to be part of
a letter; a 'long' or possibly an 'acute'

2804. Sophocles?

There are reasons for entertaining the notion that the following remnant of a play
may represent the *Acrisius* of Sophocles, but the argument is weak (*v.* Fr. 1, 27 n.) and
there are considerations which make against both the identification of the play and the
attribution of these verses to Sophocles. First, the correspondence (on which the
identification turns) between Fr. 1, 27 and the quotation from Sophocles (and not
improbably, but not certainly, from his *Acrisius*) in Hesychius is extremely inexact.
Secondly, no detail is recognizable which can be referred specifically to any part of the
story of Acrisius. (But I do not think that anything should be made of the incongruity
with a legendary story of Lydian scent, Sardian rug, and perhaps some object from
Tarentum; the absurdity is no greater than that of Ἰϲτριανίδων ὕφη γυναικῶν in the
Eurypylus, fr. 210, 67 seq. P.) Thirdly, suspicion attaches to the ending of Λυδικόν as
a Sophoclean form and to a lesser degree to μέϲωϲ (if it occurs) and ἄκρηβον as constituents of the Sophoclean vocabulary.

The hand is a neat upright example of the angular type and may, I suppose, be
dated in the later part of the second century. As far as I can tell, most of the lection
signs might be by the same hand as the text, but a different pen seems to have written
the sign in Fr. 1, 20 and βι in l. 27 and perhaps the first ι in Fr. 2 (*a*) ii 3 as well as one
or two of the accents.

Fr. 1   Fr. 2 (*a*)

       Col. i   Col. ii

```
        ]ξυνἐῖναικ[           ]τηι·           εχουϲαδ..[
        ]..μα.οϲδε·κ[         ]ᾱι                 [   ]φευ[
        ]ηφανειϲθαι[          ]               κεχρειμενη[   ]μαιϲεβ[
        ]ϲικαιμεγιϲτ[         ]               ἠλυδικονβ.ενθε.[]νἠ.[
  5     ]παρτ[.]ατιν.[        ]                    οπω[].ε.[.]..[      5
        ]ηνγαμηλέ[                          ο[.]κ.υν.[].ε[]δ'αν..[].[.].[
        ]οχλοϲτυραν[          ]ϲαϲ..          .[   ]ων.ν[]..[]καταρ..ϲα[
        ]ρακώθηϲυ.[           ]              .[   ]αϲανενταπητιϲαρδ[
        ]νελουϲατα[                          ].ελευ[.]ᾱιχειριχα.[
  10    ]ανηθελουϲ[                          ].ων..[   ].οιϲυδαϲι.[    10
        ].νφρενων[                           ]α..[].[   ]αιταραντ.[
        ]αμενταδω[                           ]ο...[   ]ζώϲτοιϲιϲυ[
        ]υδεν[].κεικ.[      Fr. 2 (b)              ]ϲϲοῠκαιφ[]λ[
        ]δε...νουκ[            .                    ]εινμ.ν.εν[
  15    ].απαντων[          ]ν.[                    ]δά..[].δε.[        15
        ]λουτοϲειημα[       ]..ρ[                   ].ν.[
        ]γλυκειαννυ[          .     .                ]ην[
        ]νάκρηβονα[
        ]νκομιζειν.[
  20    ]ωιμοι     .[
        ]νμεϲωϲεχο[
        ]...εμνυκτη[
        ]αποκτενε[
        ]αϲτ.νῆκα[
  25  ].[   ].[   ]χουϲαν[
        ]ευδαιμον[
    ].ιϲψᾱλεῖβιδυνη[
```

Fr. 1 1 seq. Below ξ a trace which might be the upper end of an acute (not, I think, the right-hand end of a *paragraphus*)   2]..., if two letters, ι preceded at more than the usual interval by the middle of a stroke descending from left, but I am inclined to think that a single μ may be the likeliest interpretation of the traces   Between α and ο a dot on the line, below and to left of ο; κ, λ, or χ seems likeliest   3 αι[, α rather anomalous, but not, I think, λ or to be combined with ι as ν[4 Of τ only the stalk   5 Of τ only the foot of the stalk   .[, γ or the left-hand part of π   7 οχλοϲ slopes upwards so that ϲ finishes well above the general level   8 Above ω the first hand wrote a flat acute on which a more sloping acute was written (by the same or another hand?)   .[, the lower part of an upright   9 Above ου a thick dot with a grave to its right; if a circumflex was intended, it has fallen out anomalously   Above α the left-hand end of an accent, I am uncertain whether acute or circumflex   11]., a trace at mid letter   13 []., a dot level with the top of the letters; if the second upright of η, no whole letter is lost between ν and κ, if ι, ε or ο may have preceded   .[, a dot on the line   14 After ε the lower part of an upright descending well below the line, followed by a faint trace on the line, and this by the foot of an upright   15]., a dot level with the top of the letters   19 .[, the upper end of a stroke descending to right and below it the start of a stroke rising to right; perhaps χ, but written below the usual level   20 .[, a letter or sign, written with a thicker pen, which I cannot interpret. It has the appearance of an upright with the left-hand part of a circumflex attached to the right-hand side of its lower end; not ⊦, ω, or κ (none of which would be relevant)   22]..., a slightly convex stroke, starting slightly above the general level and ending about mid letter, followed by what looks most like α but anomalous and perhaps corrected, and this by the upper part of a triangular letter   ϝ also is anomalous, but ο does not account for all the ink Above ϝι and the left-hand apex of μ faint traces   24 Between τ and ν a dot level with the top of the letters with a trace below at mid letter   Between ν and η a dot on the line   25].[, the foot of an upright with a trace to left   ].[, a dot level with the top of the letters   27]., γ or the right-hand angle of τ or ψ   β apparently rewritten or written on another letter. βι written with a slightly thicker pen in a space which seems to have been left for it

Fr. 2 (*a*) The cross-fibres of fr. 1 are at once recognizable in fr. 2 (*a*) but, as they dip from left to right, the position of the writing relatively to them is altered. I do not think it is to be doubted that fr. 2 (*a*) i 1 seq. contain the ends of fr. 1, 1 seq. There is a certain congruence between ξυνεῖναι (if that occurs) and -τημι, and to suppose that fr. 2 (*a*) i represents the ends of the column next after fr. 1, that is, to allow for the completion of the verses in fr. 1, the intercolumnar space, and almost the whole width of the verses contained on this hypothesis in fr. 2 (*a*) i, would make a remarkably wide 'sheet', there being no 'joint' between the left-hand edge of fr. 1 and the right-hand edge of fr. 2 ii

Col. i 2 Apparently not]ᾱ̄   6 *marg.* After cαc prima facie λ followed by a thick dot (not, I think, a small ink-filled ο). α, even if much damaged, does not seem an acceptable alternative to λ

Col. ii The right-hand side has been patched just inside the edge with a narrow strip of papyrus extending from below l. 2 to l. 15

1 ..[, a trace just below the line, followed by an upright   2 Of ϝ nothing but a dot about mid letter   3 Between ε (which appears to have been made out of an original ι) and μ an unusually long ι has been inserted (I am not sure whether by the original or by another hand)   4 After β a dot well below the line   .[], a trace just off the line, compatible with an upright, followed by a blank space from which all ink has vanished   .[, a dot about mid letter   5 Before ϝ traces compatible with ε, θ, after ϝ traces suggesting a triangular letter   [.]..[rubbed and mostly blank   6 Between κ and υ a dot at mid letter; ο probable   Between ν and ε scattered dots on a rubbed and damaged surface   ..[, the right-hand end of a cross-stroke, as of γ, followed by a short convex stroke off the line and a dot about mid letter   .[.]., a stroke descending from left, perhaps δ likeliest, followed by a blank space from which the ink has vanished, and this by the lower part of a slightly forward-sloping stroke   7 .[, the foot of an upright slightly below the line   ν.ν, there appears to be no room for the third letter, but if only νν is written there is something unaccounted for in or near the top of the second upright of the first ν   ..[, scattered traces, perhaps of three letters   After ρ a blank space somewhat greater than the usual interval between letters, followed by a stroke resembling the lower part of the right-hand stroke of α but with a cross-stroke (I am not sure whether part of the significant ink) going to right from its top—the whole now has the appearance of a flattened c at about mid letter   Before c an upright descending well below the line with a trace to right of its top   8 .[, a dot level with the top of the letters, having above and to right the left-hand end of a cross-stroke   Of ϝ only a trace of the top and the base   Of τ only the left-hand end of the cross-stroke   9]., a dot below the line and a dot, slightly to right of it, above the line   .[, the start of a stroke rising to right   10]., a dot slightly above the level of ω   .[, the right-hand stroke of a triangular letter, δ or λ rather than α, followed by the start of a stroke rising to right   ]., the left-hand apex and tip of the right-hand upright of μ or ν   .[, the left-hand side of a small circle on the line   11 ..[, a trace on the line, followed by the tip of an upright having close to its right-hand side what looks like an apex formed by two strokes which diverge lower down   ].[, a dot well above the general level of the letters   .[, perhaps the back of ε   12 ...[, perhaps the top and bottom of c, followed by the top

and left-hand arc of a circle, possibly θ, and this by the top of a loop, with a trace of a cross-stroke below its right-hand edge .[, the left-hand part of μ or ν 13 Between ϕ and λ a blank sufficient for one broad or perhaps two narrow letters 14 Between μ and ν perhaps a damaged ϵ, though ι might be a more natural interpretation of the ink Between ν and ϵ the middle part of an upright perhaps with traces of a cross-stroke to right of its top, i.e. γ 15 ..[, triangular letters; prima facie, $\lambda\delta$, but the surface is rubbed and the remains of ink may be deceptive []. a blank followed by ink which looks like the top of an upright to which is attached by the upper end of its left-hand arm the upper part of ν; this is above the general level and more than the usual distance from δ .[, the top of an upright, perhaps having ink to right of its tip, but I think the appearance is caused by darkening of the surface 16]., the edge of an upright .[, prima facie, a headless c followed by a thick dot on the line and the start of a stroke rising to right

Fr. 2 (*b*) The cross-fibres fix this scrap at the level shown. I cannot follow the vertical fibres, but there is a strong general resemblance between this and the left-hand piece of the two of which fr. 2 (*a*) ii is made up

1 .[, the lower part of an upright 2].., the lower end of an upright descending well below the line, followed by the extreme top of a small circle level with the top of the letters

Fr. 1 1–19 The simplest and, I should say, likeliest hypothesis is that these are the left-hand sections of iambic trimeters lacking about four letters, and nowhere more than two syllables, at the beginning. But I see no certainty that they are in this, or even that they are all in one and the same, metre. Whether there is more than one speaker is likewise uncertain.

]ξυνεῖναι may be supplemented and articulated in more than one way. If ξυνεῖναι is to be recognized (as I should guess from the apparent dative]τηι in fr. 2 (*a*) i 1), the smooth breathing may have been intended to preclude ξυνεῖναι, 'to understand'.

5 C]παρτ[ι]ᾶτιν.

6 No word beginning with γαμηλε- is recorded except γαμήλευμα, Aesch. *Choeph.* 624. This, I suppose, implies the possible existence of a verb γαμηλεύω (formed like νοcηλεύω) and the marginal entry, fr. 2 (*a*) i 6, might well be the ending of an aorist participle. Apart from some such explanation, there seems nothing for it but to postulate the writing of -ει- for -ι-.

7 Of the three words available, ὄχλος, κόχλος, μόχλος, the last has an obvious application to the story of Danae, imprisoned by her father, Acrisius.

8 -ανθρακόω, -ρακόω, -οστρακόω, seem to be the only choices. The first occurs in the dramatists in the perfect participle passive of the simple verb (Aesch. *P.V.* 372, Eur. *Cycl.* 614) and compounded with κατά (Aesch. *Orith.* fr. 281, 4 N²; Soph. *El.* 58, Eur. *Cycl.* 663, *I.A.* 1602; all middle or passive) and ἐξ (Ion *Omph.* fr. 28 N²; active); κατερρακωμένος (Soph. *Trach.* 1103) and ὀcτρακουμένη (Aesch. *Ostol.* fr. 80, 4 N²) are the only examples of the other two.

9 (-)ελοῦcα presumably indicated.

18 ἄκρηβον not again till Theoc. viii 93.

20 This spelling (as against ὤμοι) is referred to in *Et. Mag.* 822 in ὤμοι and is found sporadically over a long period; e.g. Sappho 94, 4, *Il.* i 149 (codd. A, B, C), Aesch. *Pers.* 253 (cod. M), Soph. *Aj.* 946 (cod. L), Aristoph. *Nub.* 925 (cod. R). The ι is not always reported.

21 μέcωc (if the letters are so to be articulated) not in Aeschylus or Sophocles; three instances in Euripides. But ἐν μέcωι is common in all three tragedians.

27 ψαλεῖ βίδυν: Hesych. in βίδην has: εἶδος. κροῦμα. Cοφοκλῆς ἀκρίτως [Βηρcαβεέ—Παλαιcτίνης] ὡc ἐπιψάλλ( ) βίδηνται καὶ ξυναυλίαν. ἄλλοι βίθυν; and in βυδοί· οἱ μουcικοί. ἢ κρούμά τι coφῶc κρηcίν. From these entries there has been elicited a quotation from the *Acrisius* of Sophocles, ὡc ἐπιψάλλειν βίδην τε καὶ ξυναυλίαν (fr. 60 P), in which βίδυν may be substituted from the present text. The question is whether the two verses may reasonably be supposed to be the same. I should say, it must be judged impossible. On the other hand, it seems to me a plausible hypothesis that both came from the same play and referred to the same occasion, though I am bound to add that there are details about this text which raise the suspicion that it may be by a writer later than Sophocles, who may have copied the locution ψάλλειν βίδυν, or the locution may not have been as rare as it now appears to us.

Fr. 2 (*a*) Col. ii 3 κεχριμένη[is ambiguous. From the context I presume the sense here to be 'anointed' and one would then look for a dative of that with which the anointing is done. If this dative is contained in]μαις, I can find nothing better than ὀδμαῖς, which appears to be used of material scents at any rate as early as Eur. *Phaethon* (κἀπιχωρίοις ὀςμαῖςι θυμιῶςιν εἰςόδους fr. 773, 14 N²). But in view of the presence of β[and of Λυδικόν in the next verse, it may be worth while to mention the possibility that the required dative was β[ακκάρει (Achae. Αἴθ. fr. 10 N² β. χριςθέντα, or β[ακκάριδι, Magnes Λυδ. fr. 3 N² β. κεχριμένον). This Lydian scent, which is referred to by a number of early authors (e.g. Semon. fr. 14, Hipponax 2175 fr. 3, 11 seqq.), was certainly mentioned by Sophocles (fr. 1032 P, and, for that matter, by Aeschylus Ἀμυμ. fr. 14 N² and Ion 'Ομφ. fr. 24 N²).

Below the beginning of this line the overlayer is destroyed, but I am fairly sure that, if a *paragraphus* had been written, it would still be visible.

4 ἢ Λυδικὸν βρένθει[ο]ν . . . (whether affirmative or interrogative) looks reasonably secure.

Λυδικόν is unexpected. The adjective is Λυδός or Λύδιος in the three tragedians (as also in Ion) and I think it may be said that with a few exceptions (for instance, Ἑλληνικός) the extension of κτητικά in -ικός is prose, comic, or earlier or later.

βρένθειον μύρον τῶν παχέων ὡς ἡ βάκκαρις, οἱ δὲ ἀνθινὸν μύρον Et. Mag. 212, 41 = Bekk. Anecd. 223, 10, and the like in other lexica. The word appears, prima facie as an adjective, in Sappho fr. 94, 19, as a noun in Pherecrates Λήρ. fr. 173 K. It was not hitherto specifically said to be Lydian.

5 I suppose ὅπω[ς] θελ . . .

6 ο[ὐ]κουν.

8 Λυδικόν above makes Cαρδ[ιανικῶι (cf. Aristoph. *Ach.* 112, *Pax* 1174) unobjectionable here and I suppose there can be no doubt that a Sardian rug was mentioned, though it would be possible to find a different way of expressing its provenance. For these cf. Heracl. ἐν ᾱ Περςικῶν (ap. Athen. 514 c διῄιει . . . πεζὸς ὑποτιθεμένων ψιλοταπίδων Cαρδιανῶν), Clearchus ἐν . . . Γεργιθίωι (ap. Athen. 255 c κλίνης ὑπεςτρωμένης Cαρδιανῆι ψιλοτάπιδι τῶν πάνυ πολυτελῶν), Varro *Herc. Socrat.* (ap. Non. Marc. 539, 542 cubo in Sardianis tapetibus).

9 Apparently λευ[κ]ᾶι χειρί, and therefore in a choric part. (τελευτᾶι is not a possible reading.)

11 If Ταραντ.[is to be recognized—there are other possible articulations—there might be a reference to something of the same sort as the Ταραντῖναι βαφαί, purple clothes, apparently mentioned by Achaeus (fr. 40 N²). But Ταραντι[does not seem to have been written; Ταραντε[ι may have been.

2805. PLAY

The obvious source of the following fragment is a tragedy or satyr play. In ll. 4–7 one character seems to be recommending another to hurry after a female hiding in the house. The following lyric, so far as I can tell, contains a foreboding of rape and murder.

Lines 4–7 would naturally be taken for iambic trimeters, and so they may be, but the hypothesis is not without difficulties. L. 7 lacks two syllables, ll. 4–6 only one; I can suggest no probable supplements which would bring all their left-hand edges into alignment. If the lines were trochaic tetrameters, enough elbow-room would be won to escape these difficulties, but besides any general improbability there are two particular objections, (a) that l. 6 would exhibit a scansion found in only two other places, (b) that the depth of the εἴςθεςις of ll. 8–11 would be inordinately great.

The writing is a careful rounded upright bookhand of medium size, to be assigned, I suppose, to the early second century. The four accents appear to be due to the copyist.

      ·   ·

]ε[

].[

]ουϲα . αιδοϲηχω [

]αιϲεκεινηντηνφοβουμενηνεϲω   [

5   ] . νενπιθῶνικαπικυψελαιϲκρυφῆι   [

]νηνκαταπτηϲϲουϲανο[.] . ενειϲταχυν   [

]νκαταυτηντπρινκεκρυμμενηνλαθειν   [

]   απαπαιε[]ε   [

]   βραχυτιτουγμεϲωιδιοιϲειγοναϲ   [

10   ]   μοροϲαπαρ[.]ενῳ[. . . .]ματοιϲκοραιϲ[

]επιμεγατο . εφλ[ ]κον   [

The text is on two separate pieces. The inside edge, particularly of the left-hand piece, is apt to be ragged and twisted

3 The first α represented only by the lower end of the right-hand stroke; λ possible   The second α represented by the lower part of the right-hand stroke and part of the cross-stroke; anomalous, but not δ   5]., a dot level with the top of the letters   The last ι curves backwards and in other circumstances might have been taken for υ   6]., the upper part of a slightly convex upright 11 Between ο and ε a speck on the line to left of the gap and a flat stroke, its right-hand end hooked under to left, on the line to right of the gap

3 If παιδὸϲ (which I can in no way verify) ἠχώ, the nearest parallel I can find is Alc. 130 34 ἄχω . . . γυναίκων. Eur. *Hipp.* 791 ἠχὼ . . . προϲπόλων is called in question by the latest editor. In a number of analogous passages ἠχώ has been displaced by critics in favour of ἠχή, e.g. ϲάλπιγγοϲ ἠχώ Eur. *Troad.* 1267 (ἠχήν Pierson), τῶνδ' ἀνακτόρων ἄπο ἠχοῦϲ ἰούϲηϲ Eur. *Suppl.* 88 seq. (ἠχῆϲ Nauck).

4 The most probable articulation and interpretation seems -αιϲ, the person addressed being the same as in l. 6 -ενειϲ. θηρᾶιϲ, for instance, does not look incompatible with the context; cf. θηρῶντεϲ Ἑλένην Eur. *Troad.* 369. φωρᾶιϲ might be another possibility.

ἔϲω 'within (the house)', as, e.g., Aesch. *Cho.* 921 ἡμένας ἔϲω.

5 If the line is an iambic trimeter, I can make no satisfactory suggestion for the lost syllable. ν]ῦν appears to be admissible as a reading.

ἐν πιθῶνι πιθών is a place where πίθοι are stored: τὰϲ . . . ἀποθήκας τοῦ οἴνου Ξενοφῶν μὲν οἰνῶναϲ εἴρηκεν Εὔπολις δὲ πιθῶναϲ Pollux vi 15. If ἐπὶ κυψέλαιϲ is to be parallel, it must be taken, not as 'on (the) boxes', but as 'in the box-room'. For this I should have expected ἀμφί in preference to ἐπί, and from καί, not ἤ, infer that jars and chests were kept in the same place.

5 seq. κρυφῆι . . . καταπτήϲϲουϲαν, 'cowering in hiding'. Cf. Aesch. *Eum.* 252 ἐνθάδ' ἐϲτί που καταπτακών (this and καταπτήξω Soph. fr. 442 P l. 8 the only instances of καταπτήϲϲω in the tragedians).

6 An argument against supposing ll. 4–7 trochaic tetrameters is the consequent necessity of admitting in this line a scansion found only twice in the tragedians, at Aesch. *Pers.* 165 and Soph. *Phil.* 1402. If only one syllable is lost at the beginning, one of the possibilities to be considered is that -νην represents the object of καταπτήϲϲουϲαν. Of this it has to be said that it is a construction found later and in prose, but not in the tragedians, who, however, offer ὑποπτήϲϲω (-ειν . . . θεούϲ Aesch. *P.V.* 960, -ων χόλον ibid. 29) and πτήϲϲω (ἀπειλὰϲ πτήξας ibid. 174[1]) so used.

6 seq. ο[ὐ] ϲενεῖϲ? The sense required seems to be 'hurry after her before she is hidden and cannot be found'. This might be expressed by something like οὐ ϲενεῖϲ ταχὺν δρόμον κατ' αὐτὴν πρὶν κεκρυμμένην λαθεῖν;

[1] But some doubt attaches to this example. At Soph. *Ichn.* 1174 vi 19 seq. οὐδὲ ψόφοιϲι. . . . πτήϲϲοντοϲ exhibits the more naturally expected construction.

οὐ τενεῖς; as imperative, v. Kühner–Gerth i 176 or Gildersleeve, *Syntax* i § 271.

ταχύν I suppose implies some word for 'pursuit', 'search' or the like. I can suggest nothing better than δρόμον, but I can adduce no stronger support than the Homeric ἵπποιϲι τάθη δρόμοϲ *Il.* xxiii 375, τοῖϲι . . . τέτατο δρόμοϲ *ibid.* 758 (= *Od.* viii 121). A parallel of a sort may be seen in Eur. *Hec.* 271 ποῖον ἁμιλλῶμαι λόγον; *Hel.* 546 ὄρεγμα δεινὸν ἡμιλλημένην. On this hypothesis κατ' αὐτήν will be 'on her track'. There are several examples of κατά so used in Herodotus, e.g. iii 4, ix 53, but I can find none in tragedy except Soph. fr. 812 (898 Pearson; see his note).

If the line were a tetrameter, something like ϲτέγην κατ' αὐτήν would seem apposite, but I have no satisfying suggestion for the preceding cretic. 'In the house itself' opposed to standing here in the street.

8–10 Dochmiacs.

8 ἀπαπαπαῖ ἐέ: similarly Aesch. *Agam.* 1114 ἐέ παπαῖ παπαῖ, Eur. *Hippol.* 594 αἰαῖ ἐέ.

9 seq.   βραχύ τι τοὐν μέϲωι διοίϲει γονᾶϲ
                          μόροϲ ἀπ' ἀρ[ϲ]ένω[ν ἀδα]μάτοιϲ κόραιϲ.

If this is a single complete sentence, it is susceptible of translation as: By a small amount between will doom at the hand of males differ from childbirth for virgin girls. But βραχύ τι τὸ ἐν μέϲωι· might be an independent sentence of the same kind as οὐ πολλὸν τὸ μεϲηγύ· at Theogn. 553. Cf. Eur. *Alc.* 914.

βραχύ τι, more or less equivalent to ὀλίγον, is found in comedy (Aristoph. *Thesmoph.* 398, Plat. com. Φάων fr. 175, 2) and prose (Thuc. vi 12, Plat. *Rep.* vi 496 Β, *al.*), but tragedy exhibits only βραχύ (Soph. *Trach.* 415, *Electr.* 1304; Eur. *Ion* 744, *al.*), except that at Eur. *Stheneb.* 14 the unmetrical πειϲθείϲ τι βραχύ is the reading of the MS.

τοὐν μέϲωι: τοι[1] appears to me more appropriate than το. At Eur. *Aeolus* fr. 27, 1 ἦ βραχύ τοι ϲθένοϲ ἀνέροϲ.

With ὀλίγον διαφέρει τί τινοϲ there is properly no place for ἐν μέϲωι, but a comparable superfluity is seen in Eur. *Ion* 1284 τί δ' ἐϲτὶ Φοίβωι ϲοί τε κοινὸν ἐν μέϲωι;

διοίϲει: διαφέρειν in the sense of 'be different from' not in Aeschylus or Sophocles, once in Euripides (*Orest.* 251) and not out of the way in comedy (usually in negative or interrogative sentences, e.g. Aristoph. *Nub.* 503, 1428, Cratin. *Nem.* fr. 108) and prose. Eur. *Troad.* 1248 τοῖϲ θανοῦϲι διαφέρειν βραχύ, εἰ . . . may be mentioned for its verbal similarity, but it exemplifies a use quite different from what is postulated here.

γονᾶϲ: γονή in the sense of 'parturition' is not very common in tragedy. *Phoen.* 355 δεινὸν γυναιξὶν αἱ δι' ὠδίνων γοναί, *Ion* 328 θέϲπιϲμα παιδῶν ἐϲ γονάϲ may be adduced from Euripides. I have no instance of the singular, unless it occurred at Eur. fr. 839 ἀπ' αἰθερίου βλαϲτόντα γονῆϲ. τόκου would have been easier to interpret.

μόροϲ ἀπ' ἀρϲένων: cf. ἀπ' Ἀργείαϲ χερὸϲ τέθνηκα Eur. *Orest.* 1027, τῆι ἀφ' ὑμῶν τιμωρίαι Thuc. i 69, ἀδῆιον ϲπαρτῶν ἀπ' ἀνδρῶν Soph. *O.C.* 1533 seq.

ἄρϲην used by all three tragedians as a synonym of ἀνήρ, e.g. μετ' ἀρϲένων ψῆφον ἔθεντ' ἀτιμώϲαντεϲ ἔριν γυναικῶν Aesch. *Suppl.* 643 seq., ἀρϲένων . . . κλαγγά Soph. *Trach.* 206 seq., χεῖρον' ἀρϲένων νόϲον ταύτην νοϲοῦμεν Eur. *Androm.* 220 seq.[2] In Eur. *Melanipp. Desm.* fr. 499, 1 seqq. εἰϲ γυναῖκαϲ ἐξ ἀνδρῶν ψόγοϲ is taken up by αἱ δ' εἰϲ ἀμείνουϲ ἀρϲένων. The facts are not made clear in the LSJ article.

ἀδαμάτοιϲ: cf. Aesch. *Suppl.* 143 = 153 εὐνὰϲ ἀνδρῶν ἄγαμον ἀδάμα{ν}τον ἐκφυγεῖν, Soph. *Aj.* 450 ἀδάμα{ϲ}τοϲ θεά (Athena).

11 I should have guessed ἐπὶ μέγα τόδε φλέγει κακόν, but [εγεικα] seems too long for the space, and even if another form of φλέγειν a letter shorter is chosen, there would still be hardly enough room.

If ἐπὶ μέγα 'to a great extent, to a high degree', it has parallels (Thuc. i 118, 2; ii 97, 5) and many analogies (e.g. ἐπὶ βραχύ Thuc. i 118, 2; ἐπὶ μεῖζον Thuc. iv 117; ἐπὶ πᾶν Xen. *Anab.* iii 1, 18) in prose, and analogies (though I think they are rarer) in verse, such as ἐπὶ ϲμικρόν S. *Electr.* 414, ἐπὶ μεῖζον S. *Phil.* 259, but I can find no other instance in the tragedians of ἐπὶ μέγα itself.

---

[1] τοι is not always easy to recognize. At Aesch. *Agam.* 242 I should write θὼϲ (θ' ὼϲ M).

[2] As the meaning seems to be, not 'we suffer in this a worse sickness than men', but 'we suffer this sickness but worse than men', I should have thought χεῖρον more logical than χεῖρον(α).

At Aesch. *Agam.* 260 I believe the truth to be that ἄρϲενοϲ is the genitive dependent on ἐρημωθείϲ, and not either the genitive dependent on θρόνοϲ or the genitive of ἄρϲην θρόνοϲ.

2806. OLD COMEDY

Although the contents of Fr. 1 i of the following manuscript should make it possible to identify their source, if any record of it had been otherwise preserved, I have found nothing suitable among the fragments of Old Comedy and no name of a play to suggest that this prophecy might have been a feature of it. The only clue is that μετεκβάλλειν occurs nowhere in Greek but here, but that Cratinus used the derived noun.

The text is placed within lavish margins both between columns and below. It may be worth noting that fr. 1, more than 13½ in. wide, is a single sheet without joints. The hand is a medium-sized slightly sloping example of the well-represented angular type which I should have referred to the third century but that the note at fr. 1 i 10 looks to me like second-century writing. The two or three corrections might be attributable to this pen, the lection signs apparently to a finer point.

Fr. 1

Col. i

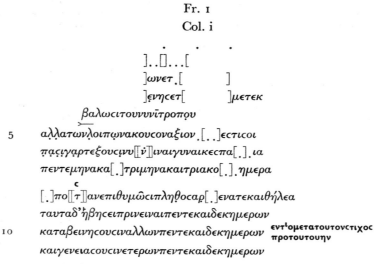

```
            ].. .[          .
          ]ωνετ.[              ]
          ]ενηϲετ[        ]μετεκ
      βαλωϲιτουννυνῑτροπου
   5  αλλατωνλοιπωνακουϲοναξιον.[..]εϲτιϲοι
      παϲιγαρτεξουϲιννυ[[ν̅]]ιναιγυναικεϲπα[.].ια
      πεντεμηνακα[.]τριμηνακαιτριακο[.].ημερα
                      ϲ
      [.]πο[[τ]]ανεπιθυμωϲιπληθοϲαρ[.]ενατεκαιθηλεα
      ταυταδ᾽ηβηϲειπρινειναιπεντεκαιδεκημερων
  10  καταβεινηϲουϲιναλλωνπεντεκαιδεκημερων   εντ᾽ομετατουτονϲτιχοϲ
                                               προτουτουην
      καιγενειαϲουϲινετερωνπεντεκαιδεκημερων
```

Fr. 1 Col. i 1]..[, the foot of an upright, followed by the lower part of an upright descending below the line; perhaps a single π possible   ]...[, a dot on the line, the lower part of an upright descending well below the line, the start of a stroke on the line   2 .[, perhaps ο followed by the tail of a stroke curling up to right; resembles ω but not the ω of this hand

Fr. 1 Col. i L. 4 is an acatalectic iambic dimeter. There is no telling what preceded, but the projection of l. 3 beyond the end of l. 2 shows that more than one metre was represented.

Ll. 5–11 are catalectic trochaic tetrameters. But for the first of these lines, it would be reasonable to recognize an address of the audience by the chorus, that is, to take them for part of the παράβαϲιϲ of the play, the ἐπίρρημα and ἀντεπίρρημα of the παράβαϲιϲ of at any rate an Aristophanic comedy being characterized by the use of this metre.

The address of a single person in l. 5 appears to be inconsistent with this hypothesis. In fact, I can think of no explanation of the transition from the singular to the plural unless ϲοι refers to some collective noun, e.g. δῆμοϲ or πόλιϲ. In that case, this might still be the ἀντεπίρρημα of a παράβαϲιϲ.

Fr. 1

Col. i

3   ̔μετεκ-

βάλωςι τοῦ νυνὶ τρόπου.

5 ἀλλὰ τῶν λοιπῶν ἄκουςον, ἄξιον γ[άρ] ἐςτί ςοι.

πᾶςι γὰρ τέξουςιν ὑμῖν αἱ γυναῖκες πα[ι]δία

πεντέμηνα κα[ὶ] τρίμηνα καὶ τριακο[ν]τήμερα.

[ὅ]πός’ ἂν ἐπιθυμῶςι πλῆθος, ἄρ[ρ]ενά τε καὶ θήλεα.

ταῦτα δ’ ἡβήςει πρὶν εἶναι πεντεκαίδεκ’ ἡμερῶν

11   καὶ γενειάςουςιν ἑτέρων πεντεκαίδεκ’ ἡμερῶν

10   κᾆτα βινήςουςιν ἄλλων πεντεκαίδεκ’ ἡμερῶν

Fr. 1 Col. i 3 seq. μετεκβάλλειν is not recorded, but Cratinus is credited with μετεκβολή· μεταβολή καὶ ἐξάλλαξις (fr. 427 ap. Phot. *lex.*). μετεκβάλλειν may presumably have any of the constructions of μεταβάλλειν, which is used both transitively and intransitively. In the context a reasonable guess is that τοῦ νυνὶ τρόπου means the state *from* which the 'change' is made.

4 Cf. Thuc. i 6, 4 τὸν νῦν τρόπον, 'the present fashion'.

5 Cf. Aristoph. *Eq.* 624 ἀκοῦςαί γ’ ἄξιον τῶν πραγμάτων, and for the dative *ibid.* 616 ἄξιόν γε πᾶςίν ἐςτιν ἐπολολύξαι, Dem. *Fals. leg.* 310 οὓς ἐλεεῖν . . . ὑμῖν ἄξιον.

6 Hdt. vi 69 τίκτουςι γὰρ γυναῖκες καὶ ἐννεάμηνα καὶ ἑπτάμηνα καὶ οὐ πᾶςαι δέκα μῆνας ἐκτελέςαςαι.

7 I cannot say for certain that -θη- was not written, but the remaining ink is compatible with the foot of the stalk of τ and does not in any way suggest the base of θ. In view of the κ’ for χ’ in ll. 9–11 (which also I cannot explain), I have taken τ as the παράδοςις.

8 ὁπόςα . . . πλῆθος: cf. κόςοι πλῆθος; Hdt. i 153, πλῆθος ὡς διςχίλιοι Xen. *Anab.* iv 2, 2.

9 'Before they are a fortnight old': cf. Xen. *Memor. Socr.* i 2, 40 πρὶν εἴκοςιν ἐτῶν εἶναι. The same phrase in the next two verses contains a genitive of a different nature.

10 seq. γενειάϲουϲιν. The girls have been left behind.

ἔν τι(ϲιν) sc. ἀντιγράφοιϲ. 'In some copies these two lines are transposed.' Unless some joke that I have missed underlies the order presented by this manuscript, the alternative seems to me preferable on two grounds : (*a*) it would appear to a Greek the natural order ; see, e.g., Alc. **120** where the marginal note has ταῦτα . . . εἰρωνεῖαι εἴϲ τινα γήμαντα πρὶν γενειάϲαι, (*b*) in a sequence of three members ἕτεροϲ applies more aptly to the second and ἄλλοϲ more aptly than ἕτεροϲ to the third.

ἡμερῶν: the common genitive of time within which, 'in the next fortnight', cf., e.g., Hdt. vi 58 ἐπέαν θάψωϲι, ἀγορὴ δέκα ἡμερέων οὐκ ἵϲταταί ϲφι.

Fr. 1

Col. ii

    .   .   .   .

     ⟦.⟧.ω[

     λε..[   ]υχα[

     αναμ[   ]μελ[

     επιτρ[   ]υμ[   ]νο.[

5   εγγυτ[   ].ν[.]υϲ.[   ]εα..[

        π..τανεμ[.]..βιαϲ[

        τέμενοϲμ[.]γακαι[

        πλατυ,πιϲτοναπαϲι..[Fr. 2

        ϊδρυϲαϲθεφρενωνϋπ[.   .   .

10   περιδαυτοδικαιων[   ].νπρο⟦ϲ⟧ἑδρ[

        επιπαϲιμενεργοιϲ [   ]ωντουϲφιλ[

        επιπαϲ[.]δεμυθοιϲ [   ].αταφαγειν[

Col. ii 1 ⟦.⟧., the lower part of an upright hooked to right, cancelled by a diagonal stroke, ϲ apparently likelier than ε, followed by the lower part of an upright descending well below the line 2 ..[, a dot level with the top of the letters and two dots side by side below it on the line, followed by a faint trace on the line   4 .[, a speck on a single fibre about mid letter   5 The *diple obelismene* represented only by a speck of the upper arm and the right-hand end of the dash   ]., a flat stroke on the line   .[, the lower part of an upright   ..[, apparently an upright followed by another upright, but the fibres are frayed out and the ink may be displaced ; perhaps a single letter   6 After π prima facie the upper right-hand part of ο, but there are elements of an upright, descending well below the line, under its right-hand end   Before τ the upper part of a forward-sloping stroke   ].., the foot of an upright and after an interval a dot on the line ; perhaps].[.].[should be written   8 ..[, two dots on the line, some way apart

Col. ii The only two certainly complete verses, of which therefore the metre is assured, are 11 seq. These are anapaestic penthemimers, like Aristoph. *Av.* 1318 seq. = 1330 seq. It is natural to see the same in l. 10, but I do not see how this metrical view is compatible with the requirements of language.

L. 7, if complete, as prima facie it may be taken to be, is an anapaestic monometer ; l. 8 is then either an anapaestic tripody or, as I suppose more likely, dimeter.

τέμενος μ[έ]γα καὶ [

πλατύ, πιστὸν ἅπαςι . . [

ἰδρύςαςθε φρενῶν ὕπ[

10   περὶ δ' αὐτὸ δικαιων[

ἐπὶ πᾶςι μὲν ἔργοις

ἐπὶ πᾶςι δὲ μύθοις.

7 seqq. τέμενος apparently metaphorical. I suppose the object of ἰδρύςαςθε, and what is referred to in αὐτό.

9 ὕπ[appears most likely to represent ὑπό or ὑπέρ in anastrophe, though these are not the only possibilities. I can suggest nothing better than that the 'spacious reserve' is (or, is to be) 'established in your breasts', φρενῶν ὕπο.

10 seqq. 'In all deeds, in all words': αἰδὼς ἐπ' ἔργοις πᾶςι Soph. *O.C.* 1268. The mention of a person seems to be implied.

Fr. 2 1]., an upright   3]., scattered specks; no letter verifiable

Fr. 2 1 προεδρ[ίαν.

2 τοὺς φίλ[ους.

3 καταφαγεῖν, though κ not verifiable.

2807. Old Comedy, Ὧραι?

The largest of the following fragments contains a word quoted from the Ὧραι of Cratinus. This word, ὡράιζεϲθαι, would be apt to occur in comedy[1] and is in fact quoted also from Eupolis. But the triple occurrence in its immediate neighbourhood of cases of ὧραι suggests the possibility that there is some relevance to the title of the play. Nothing is known of the theme of the Ὧραι of Cratinus and I can follow no thread of meaning in what is preserved of this ms. Aristophanes also wrote a Ὧραι, of which a fragment is quoted by Athenaeus, containing (as it seems) a discussion between two Seasons about the advantages of the Athenian climate.

The hand is a fair-sized example of a well-represented type of upright uncial, comparable with **844** and PSI 1212 and to be dated early in the second century. PSI 1212, Cratinus Πλοῦτοι, is adequately supplied with lection signs. **2807**, apart from a couple of apostrophes, offers a bare text.

	Fr. 1	Fr. 2	Fr. 3
	]．ιν：ηλθετιϲδιφ．[	．η^μοιον[	]γενε．[
	]．'ανθρωποϲηλ[	ωϲα．[	]ακοτ[
	]τερονοιχετα[	εγωδ．[	]．[]ευϲα[
	]ϲθαικαιγα．．ον．[	θαϲϲ．[	]ικηλ[
5	]νεφαϲκεταυτα̣[	5 ινατι[	5]εμε[
	]．ν̣[．．]λωϲινα．．[	[	
	]ο．[．]ϲτωπαντ[	[	
	]．ε[．]αϲεμνη．ο．[		
	]τναδεκα̣．δ．ωνθηλ．[		
10	]τνιααιδοι．．δι[．]εκο．[		
	]μηνατεχνωϲγ'εϲτ[		
	]ντ̣αϲδεπεμο．και．[		
	]κλαϲθηναικαπι[		
	]．νιϲθηναι [		
15	]．ληνγευχεικατα．[		
	]．[]φιλαιπολλαϲ．[		
	]ελθεινωραϊζομενο[		
	]ωνωρεω̆ετεραϲωραϲ[		
	]．νωρεων [		
20	]ουθαρρων [		

[1] It is conjectured at Aristoph. *Eccles*. 202.

Fr. 1 1]., on the line the right-hand end of a stroke coming from left; perhaps μ likeliest .[, the upper left-hand arc of a circle   2]., the right-hand end of a cross-stroke level with the top of the letters with a speck on the line below; neither γ nor τ suggested   4 After ᾳ the extreme lower end, below the line, of a stroke hooked to right   Before ο the lower part of a stroke descending from left, having a projection to right near its top; above, ink not suggesting an accent but the upper end of a stroke descending, with a slight convex curve, to left   .[, the start of a stroke rising to right, followed by the lower left-hand arc of a small circle; λ or μ?   6 ..[, triangular letters   8]., a dot level with the top of the letters and a hook to right below on the line   Of]ᾳ only the feet   After η what looks like the cross-stroke of τ but with no trace of an upright   .[, a dot level with the top of the letters   9 Between ᾳ and δ the tips of two uprights   Before ω a serif to left below the line .[, the left-hand side of υ perhaps likeliest   10 ν ια ι inserted, apparently by the writer   Between οι and δ ink which I cannot reconcile with parts of any letters of this hand : at mid letter a cross-stroke with a thick upright at its left-hand end and a thin convex stroke at its right-hand end, followed by what resembles a reversed comma on the line with a trace to left and a trace to right level with the top of the letters   .[, the left-hand end of a cross-stroke level with the top of the letters   12 After ρ a speck just off the line   .[, the foot of an upright strongly serifed to left   14]., the lower left-hand arc of a circle   15]., a speck below the line   .[, an upright strongly serifed to left 16 .[, an upright with top hooked to left   19]., on the line a flat stroke with a short tail at its left-hand end

Fr. 2 1 *marg.* The first letter is prima facie α, but this does not account for a speck between the end points of the two sides. But it does not look as if this trace could have formed part of the base of δ 2 .[, the upper right-hand part of a loop   3 .[, a dot off the line   4 .[, the left-hand arc of a circle; I think ο, not ω

Fr. 3 1 .[, an upright   3]., the lower end of a stroke descending from left   ι, not more, might be missing in the gap between this and ε

Fr. 1 1 The inserted colon indicates a change of speaker.

8 Up to this verse the remains seem to be reconcilable with iambic trimeters, from here on with anapaestic dimeters (monometers 14, 19 seq.).

μέ[γ]α cεμνή: cf. ὦ μέγα cεμναὶ Νεφέλαι Aristoph. *Nub.* 291. As presumably there was no hiatus intended, the sign between η and ο represents a consonant, but none has been completed.

9 I suppose (ὦ) πό]τνα, though this is not a form to be expected in comedy, except in some relation (quotation, parody) to a more elevated kind of verse. πο]τνα was first written in l. 10 also, but has been converted to the regular form.

κανδρων would, I think, be acceptable, but I cannot verify it. A reference to a particular ten men (e.g. those mentioned in Thuc. viii 67; Aristot. Ἀθ. Πολ. 29, 2, or the ten generals listed by Androtion, Schol. Aristid. 485) would presumably require the article.

10 In Aristophanes always ὦ πότνια, and, except for ὦ πότνι᾿ Εἰλείθυια *Lys.* 742, *Eccles.* 369, always ὦ πότνια. There does not appear to be any particular reason for the *scriptio plena* here.

The vocative of αἰδώc being αἰδώc (ὦ πότνι᾿ Αἰδώc Eur. *Iph. Aul.* 821; fr. 436), αἰδοι must be supposed the dative αἰδοῖ or part of αἰδοῖοc.

11 καὶ μὴν ἀτεχνῶc γε . . . Aristoph. *Ran.* 106.

15 εὔχει.

17 ὡράιζεcθαι· Κρατῖνοc Ὧραιc (fr. 272), but also in Eupolis, ὡραιζομένη καὶ θρυπτομένη fr. 358.

18 seq. I do not see the reason for the Ionic forms.

2808. Comedy

Parts of iambic trimeters recognizable as belonging to a comedy, which I cannot identify but suppose to be Old more probably than New.

The writing is a fair-sized upright bookhand comparable with **1238**, which is dated about the middle of the first century.

Fr. 1

(*a*)	(*b*) Col. i	Col. ii
].εϲτοβ[	]ονεμπεϲοιϲ	ηνπουγαρῇ[
]οιπαθο[	]αρου·	ευριπιδηϲδο.[
].οπραγ.[	]ραϲω	ηνγαραταλαν η [
	]ιϲθεοιϲ·	ινακαιτρ̣ο̣ρ̣ρ̣ημ'οθεν[
5	].ϲ:ο.[ ]·	ωϲου[ ]τανμ.[
		]ημηφ[ ]ειψπα.[
		].ειουμ[
		]ημ.ν[
		]υϲ.[
10		]γε.[

Fr. 1 (*a*) There is a 'joint' at the right-hand edge

1]., γ or τ   3]., γ or τ   .[, a dot level with the top of the letters

(*b*) Col. i 5]., the upper right-hand arc of a circle

Col. ii 1 Above η the upper part of ε (or ϲ), followed by a dot or the extreme top of a small circle 2 .[, an upright with a projection to left at top   3 The τ is unusually low and may have been inserted by the original hand in a space left for it. There is a blank between ν and η not filled   4 Of ν[only the left-hand upright; μ equally possible   5 .[, the left-hand arc of a circle   6 .[, a slightly convex upright   7]., γ or τ   8 Between μ and ν the surface is stripped and only the extreme tops of strokes remain; ω may be possible, though the central apex looks anomalous 9 .[, I think, θ, but cannot rule out ε   10 .[, the top of the left-hand upright of μ or ν

Fr. 1 Col. i 1 I suppose ἐϲ τὸ β[άραθρ]ον ἐμπέϲοιϲ. As the common phrase is ἐϲ τὸ β. ἐμβάλλειν (Aristophanes four times, cf. Demiańczuk, adesp. 24, 10) ἐμπέϲοιϲ may be taken as equivalent to a passive, 'be thrown into the pit'. I have no other instance.

5 The 'colon' for a change of speaker.

Col. ii 1 ποῦ γάρ; 'certainly not'? Cf. Dem. *Pantaen.* 41. πόθεν; in a similar use, much commoner; v. Blaydes on Aristoph. *Ran.* 1455.

3 There seems to have been trouble with Ἀταλάντη (who figured, among other places, in the Μελέαγροϲ of Euripides).

Several comic poets (the majority with a good deal of uncertainty) are credited with an Ἀταλάντη. See Kock i 119 (Strattis).

Fr. 2

. . .

]μ.ρ.[
]ατο..[
]κτεκ[
]ιϲγα[
5   ]τα·κα[
]νδ᾽ετ[
]ῶϲ[

. . .

Fr. 2 1 Over μ a dot such as signifies cancellation   Before ρ only spectral remains, after ρ the lower left-hand part of ο or ϲ   2 ..[, the foot of an upright, followed by a dot on the line and this by the foot of an upright

2809. OLD COMEDY

There is no clue, that I see, to the identification of the author or source of the following scraps, and only a couple are even recognizable as from an Old Comedy.

The text is written in a medium-sized upright round bookhand rather like P. Ryl. 483 and like it probably of the second century. There are a few lection signs (apostrophes, fr. 1 i 7, fr. 2, 3, accents, fr. 1 i 7, 10, fr. 10, 2, fr. 3, 3, a rough breathing, fr. 1 i 11, a 'short', fr. 3, 3), most if not all by a different hand; the two corrections (fr. 1 i 12, fr. 7, 2) look as if they were by the same hand as the text.

Fr. 1

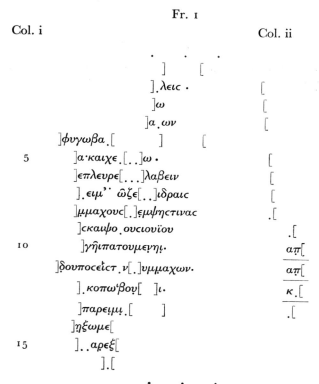

Col. i   Col. ii

```
                              ·     ·    ·
                           ]       [
                        ].λειϲ ·                    [
                        ]ω                          [
                        ]α . ων                     [
          ]φυγωβα.[        ]       [
5         ]α·καιχε.[..]ω ·                           [
          ]επλευρε[...]λαβειν                        [
          ].ειμ᾽᾽ ὦζε[..]ιδραιϲ                      [
          ]μμαχουϲ[.]εμψηϲτιναϲ                     .[
          ]ϲκαιψο.ουϲιουϊου                        .[
10        ]γῆιπατουμενηι.                          απ[
          ]δουποϲεῒϲτ.ν[.]υμμαχων.                 απ[
          ].κοπω᾽βου[ ]ι·                          κ.[
          ]παρειμι.[     ]                          .[
          ]ηξωμε[
15        ]..αρεξ[
          ].[
              ·    ·    ·
```

Fr. 1 Col. i 1]., a speck on the line   3 After α the foot of an upright   4 .[, the foot of an upright with a dot to right   5 .[, the start of a stroke rising to right; λ not much suggested   7]., a tall upright with foot hooked to right   9 Between ο and ο a speck near the line   There are two dots close together over αι; not like the *trema* following, nor a stop   11 Of δ only part of the apex and the right-hand stroke   Between τ and ν a speck, nearer ν, at mid letter   12]., the top of an upright   13 .[, the upper left-hand part of a circle; ο rather than ϲ suggested   14 η on a detached scrap, perhaps not rightly placed   15].., perhaps π preceded by a dot at the left-hand end of the cross-stroke   Of ρ only the upper right-hand side of the loop   16 The top of a circle

Col. ii 8 In the margin three dots, the second nearer to the third, and at a higher level than the others　　9 .[, converging strokes; a triangular letter or χ　　12 .[, the upper end of a stroke descending to right from the upper arm of κ　　13 .[, the upper end of a stroke descending to right

Fr. 1 Ll. 6–11 may be iambic trimeters.

5 In spite of what I say in the *app. crit.* χελ- seems unavoidable and in that case the dative of χέλειον 'shell' is the only suggestion I can make.

6 Unless a sign of elision has been omitted, or unless an Ionic form is to be allowed, an unrecorded word is represented. ὡρέων appears twice in 2807 fr. 1, 18 seq. in an otherwise Attic context.

7 ὦ Ζεῦ, τί δρᾶις;

8 ςυμμάχους πέμψηις τινάς.

9 No doubt ψόφους, though φ is unverifiable, and ψόθος also is said to mean (*inter alia*) θόρυβος, Hesych. in v., cf. Theognost. *can.* p. 54.

11 δοῦπος apparently belongs to the high style. It does not occur in comedy.
τῶν ςυμμάχων.

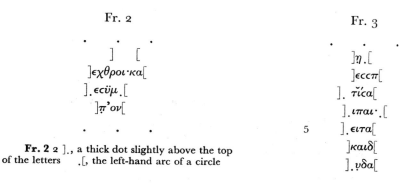

Fr. 2

]　[
]εχθροι·κα[
].εϋμ.[
]π'ον[

Fr. 3

]η.[
]εccπ[
]. τἴca[
].ιπαι·.[
5　].ειτα[
]καιδ[
].υδα[

Fr. 2 2]., a thick dot slightly above the top of the letters　　.[, the left-hand arc of a circle

Fr. 3 1 .[, the foot of an upright with a speck on the line to right; perhaps κ or ν, or two letters 3]., a slightly backward sloping upright. Between this and τ more than the normal space but no ink remaining　　4]., the tip and lower part of a stroke descending from left　　.[, a cross-stroke level with the top of the letters　　5]., the end of a cross-stroke just above the top of the letters 7]., a trace just below the general level

Fr. 4

]ιαφι[
]ονπ[
]..[

Fr. 5

]ρχαρ[
]α. [

Fr. 4 1]ι close to the edge of a stroke descending to right?　　3 .[, the tip

Fr. 6

　　　•　　•　　•

].ιδ[
]γου[

　　•　　　•

Fr. 6 1]., a speck level with the top of ι
2]χ, I think likelier than τ

Fr. 7

　•　　　•　　•

] cτερ.[
] οιο̊βο[
]υμον.[
].‥[

　　•　　•　　•

Fr. 7 Frr. 7, 8 are darker than the rest
1 .[, a speck level with the top of the letters
3 .[, the left-hand three-quarters of a circle
4 The top of a stroke suggesting α; a short flat
stroke perhaps dipping at its right-hand end; the
upper ends of two diverging strokes

Fr. 7 2 The only recorded Greek word
beginning οιοβο- is οἰοβουκόλοc, Aesch. *Suppl.* 304.
None begins οιαβο-. οἳ᾽ οβο[, οἳ᾽ ἀβο[, οἶα βο[are
manageable, but there are no signs to show they
are meant.

Fr. 8

　　•　　　•　　•

].[ ]..[
] αππα[
] εcδρ.[

　　•　　　•

Fr. 8 There is a 'joint' at the right-hand edge
1].[, the bottom left-hand arc of a circle
]..[, the right-hand end of a cross-stroke touching
near the top ε or θ　　　3 .[, the upper left-hand
arc of a circle

Fr. 8 2 ἀππα[παῖ, if this was the text, only
at Aristoph. *Vesp.* 235.

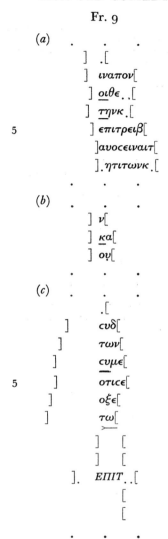

Fr. 9

(a)

    .   .   .
    ] .[
    ] ιναπον[
    ] οιθε..[
    ] τηνκ.[
5   ] επιτρειβ[
    ]ανοcειναιτ[
    ].ητιτωνκ.[

(b)

    ] ν[
    ] κα[
    ] ου[

(c)

    .[
    ] cυδ[
    ] των[
    ] cυμε[
5   ] οτιcε[
    ] οξε[
    ] τω[
    ] [
    ] [
    ]. ΕΠΙΤ..[
    [
    [

Fr. 9 Though I cannot follow the vertical fibres I am fairly confident that these fragments are from the same column. There are reasons for placing *(c)* lowest. I can see no evidence about the relative positions of *(a)*, *(b)*

(a) 3 ..[, the top of a circle, followed by the tip of an upright   4 .[, the lower left-hand arc of a circle   7]., the upper part of an upright   .[, the middle of the left-hand side of a circle

(b) 3 Of ν[only the upper end of the left-hand arm

(c) *Lower margin*]., the lower part of a stroke rising to right   ..[, an upright, damaged at the top, followed by the foot of an upright

Fr. 9 Apparently trochaic verse.

(*a*) 3 Very likely οἱ θεοί, but this is not verifiable and even these letters allow of various constructions.

5 ἐπιτρ{ε}ιβ[είης cf. Aristoph. *Thesm.* 557, *Av.* 1530. If the writing in the lower margin of (*c*) is to be read and supplemented επιτρι[β-, it looks as if there were some relation between the two occurrences, but the sign to left of επιτ‚.[is not the 'hook', ⌡, seen for instance at Bacchyl. coll. 22, 38, used to refer upwards.

6 αὖοc: see Blaydes's collections on Aristoph. *Lysist.* 385 and add Menand. *Epitrep.* 581, *Perikeir.* 163.

7 I suppose μή, though this is not immediately suggested.

Fr. 10

Scattered specks over two lines

```
        ]ερκ.[
        ]α̑ι   [
   5    ].παι [
        ]cτρο.[
        ]       [
```

Fr. 10 3 .[, the left-hand arc of a circle; though there is a trace within, I think *o* or *ω* likelier than ε　5]., specks, one just below the level of the left-hand end of the bar of π, the other on the line　　6 .[, the upper left-hand arc of a circle, φ not verifiable

Fr. 11

```
        ].ρ.γ[
        ]πυγμ[
        ] γομφ[
        ] καιγν[
   5    ] κτυπ.[
        ]αγε....[
        ]δαπαριδα[
        ].....[
```

Fr. 11 1 The first three letters are represented by ink which has soaked through on the underlayer]., α or δ　　Between ρ and γ[perhaps α acceptable　　5 seq. In the interlinear space between κ and α what now looks like an 'acute' rather than a *paragraphus*　　6 After ε the foot of an upright turning to right, followed by a dot on the line, then two traces on the line, the first apparently part of a descending, the second of a rising, stroke　　..[, the lower part of a stroke curving down from left, followed by a short arc from the lower left-hand side of a circle　　8 Of the last three letters one appears to be π, but I cannot tell whether the first or the second, and I cannot combine the remaining traces on either hypothesis

Fr. 11 2 Since the transcript was made a flake has broken off the edge of the fragment, so that the left-hand part of μ[is no longer recognizable.

Fr. 12

] [
]ταιϲτε[
]..ρυ[
].[

Fr. 12 2].., the upper end of a stroke descending to right, followed by the right-hand arc of a circle   3 The right-hand end of a cross-stroke as of γ

Fr. 13

]νδ[
]ικαπ[
]π[

Fr. 13 2 There may be a *trema* over the ι and an interlinear addition over the right-hand side of π[, but these and some other marks may be casual ink

Fr. 14

]..[
] [
].ϲκε[
]αϲ.[
5   ]α..[
]...[

Fr. 14 Partly stripped
1 A trace level with the top of the letters, followed by τ or the left-hand part of π   3]., a thick dot on the line   4 .[, the top of an upright with a projection to right near the tip
5 ..[, two uprights, the second having a stroke rising to right from its foot; if π, I cannot account for the rest   6 A short arc from the lower right-hand side of a circle, followed by the upper part of an upright; next, three traces at about mid letter

Fr. 15

]ηδ.[
]ωμ[

Fr. 15 1 .[, a slightly backward-sloping upright

Fr. 16

·   ·   ·

]κδ.[
]ματ[
].ω[

·   ·   ·

Fr. 16 1 .[, an upright with a stroke starting to right from near its top; η?   3]., γ or τ

Fr. 17

]καικο.[
]   [
]   [
]ε[

·   ·   ·

Fr. 17 1 The letters are slightly larger than the rest and the space between l. 1 and l. 4 greater than the normal allowance for three lines .[, below the line the foot of an upright turned to right

2810. Old Comedy

Not much is to be said of the fragment printed below, which is in many places uncertain or impossible of decipherment and preserves at best no more than half of the verses legible in it. Ll. 10–24 are hardly doubtfully anapaestic dimeters (which occur in various places in Aristophanic comedy), divided by a *paragraphus* into two parts of nine and six verses respectively. I can make no pretence of grasping their tenor.

The text is written in a medium-sized slightly sloping hand comparable with **1604** and P. Ryl. 529 and dated in the first half of the third century.

```
    ]       κορ . . [
    ]αι      τουϲ[
    ]        κο ιτ[
    ]—       κυδα . [
5   ] . ον . [] . .  οδε[
    ]        τ[]λαχ[
    ]      |  φιλο . [
    ]      ∫ ουδ ετ[
    ]           . αι[
10  ] . . ρωτο . . [] . cω . [
    ] . . . [] . ρονιδε . θα[              . . . [ ] . ρον ἰδέϲθα[ι
    ] . []αν . ρμη . . [] . α[             ν[]αν . ρμη . . [] . α[
    ]κ[ ] . . μετωπον[                     κ[αὶ] τὸ μέτωπον [
    ]καιτηνγαστεραφ[                       καὶ τὴν γαστέρα φ[
15  ] καιτηνκεφαλη[                        καὶ τὴν κεφαλὴ[ν
    ]ωϲτ'αποκλε . ε . ντ[                  ὥϲτ' ἀποκλείειν τ[
    ] οποτανγαρ . δημ[                     ὁπόταν γὰρ ἴδη μ[
    ]ουτωϲε . θυϲμειϲ[                     οὕτωϲ εὐθὺϲ μειϲ[
    ]τ . [ ]μη . . ρκειν[                  τ . [ ]μηδ . ρκειν[
20  ]ϋπρτ . . ηϲκαθ'ϋ . [                  ὑποτ . . ηϲ καθ' ὑ . [
    ]και . . [ . ]παιδωνο . [              καὶ τ . [ . ] παίδων ου[
    ]οιπατερ'ειπεινου[                     οἱ πατέρ' εἰπεῖν ου[
    ]ενταιϲινοδοιϲιν . [                   ἐν ταῖϲιν ὁδοῖϲιν . [
    ]καιταυταλεγουϲ'ο . [                  καὶ ταῦτα λέγουϲ' οι[
25  ] . τεραοχο  ‾‾                        
    ] . εραοχο  εμ . . . . [               εμ . . . ω[
    ] . . [ ] . . [
         .    .    .
```

C. 6233   D

In many places the surface is so rubbed that the letters have almost completely or have completely disappeared. Where the damage is less severe and scattered traces survive I have reported those that represent a restricted choice of letters

1 After ρ a triangular letter?   3 Of τ[only the left-hand end of the cross-stroke   4 Of δ only the base, of α only the apex   5 *marg.*]., on the line the turn-up of a stroke descending from left   After ν an upright against the top of its right-hand upright, followed after a blank, by a cross-stroke having ο (?) attached to its right-hand end   7 .[, a forward-sloping stroke, but ν not suggested   I see no *paragraphus*, which one would expect to find accompanying the *coronis*   9 Before α ink compatible with κ, but not suggesting it   10]., the foot of an upright, followed by an upright hooked to right at the foot; not like π as made elsewhere   After ο the foot of an upright, before c a dot on the line, about halfway between them the top of an upright   11]., two diverging strokes as of the lower part of χ   Before ρ the foot of an upright   12 ν[hardly credible, but I see no better interpretation of the ink   Between ν and ρ perhaps the top of ο   ..[, a slightly forward-sloping stroke, followed by the lower part of a second   ]., a thin stroke rising to right from below the line and having a projection to right at its middle   19 Of δ only the middle of the left-hand side and the base. The following letter is represented by a small loop, open downwards, level with the top of the letters, and a ligature to ρ   20 Between τ and η the left-hand end and the right-hand end of cross-strokes level with the top of the letters   .[, the base of a small circle and a dot above and to right above the line   21 τω[not verifiable   23 .[, an angle open to right   25 *marg. 1* Possibly]οτ or]cτ   2 Perhaps a repetition, but]τ not verifiable   After μ two forward-sloping strokes, the first having traces of a cross-stroke to right of its top, but π not suggested

2 *marg.* αι is in the hand of the text and would be expected to belong to a preceding column, which appears to be out of the question here.

5 *marg.* in a small hand may well refer to the nature of the change (e.g. of speaker) indicated by the *paragraphus* on its right.

9 Apparently ἐπείcθεcιc of a single line, unless the erasure of ink to left has been exceptionally complete.

11 λαμπρὸν ἰδέcθαι may be thought of. λ and π will pass; α is not suggested by the remaining trace; in the place of μ any letter might stand. ἰδέcθαι Aristoph. *Thesmoph.* 800.

20 The doubtful letter after τ would naturally be taken to be τ, that before η either τ or γ. There is no room for more.

25 *marg.* The note (repeated?) or notes no doubt refer to the text on their right. ὁ χο(ρóc).

2811. COMMENTARY ON AN IAMBOGRAPHER?

The scraps put together below are found on the back of a roll which contained a prose composition that I have not been able to identify. It appears to mention Λ]επτινην[, but is not part of any extant speech nor of the thirteenth Platonic letter or the fifth letter of Aeschines. This must have been a handsome manuscript, being written in a firm well-spaced bookhand comparable with **1234**. I suppose it is to be dated in the first half of the second century.

The text on the back is obviously a commentary, but it is hard to be certain on what. There are some grounds for supposing, on a verse writer, and if θεοῖcι τ' εὔχεcθαι, fr. 2, 8, was undoubtedly a lemma, there would be no question. cτυπάζει, fr. 5, 3 and 7, and κυcοδακνια[, fr. 5, 10, or κυcοκνηc[ια, fr. 5, 13, are clearly lemmata and much more likely to come from the vocabulary of verse than of prose. κυcοc and its derivatives seem to be characteristic of the Ionic, or at least not of the Attic, vocabulary.[1] On the other

---

[1] But διακυcοcαλεύων at **2743** fr. 8 ii 3, Strattis, *Λημνομέδα*.

hand, it would be expected that the crasis of τῶι αὐτῶι, fr. 5, 10, would be represented in an Ionic text by τωυτωι, but a lemma might not be accurate on such a point. But if these considerations suggest the possibility that these fragments represent another commentary on Hipponax, I can do nothing to confirm the hypothesis, and on the whole I suppose fr. 5, 7–9 must be taken to be adverse to it. Whatever it is, it is written in a hand which is a fair example of the common angular type believed to be used from the middle of the second till the fourth century. I should not suppose this specimen to fall late in the third and might even suggest the end of the second, if that did not imply a rather short life for the original contents of the roll.

Fr. 1

Col. i   Col. ii

                        ]   .[

                    ].   [
                    ].   [
                    ].c   α[
                   ]θα   5   [
5   ]φα   τ[
                   ]θε   θ.[
                   ]τ̣α   λ.[
                   ]νον   κ.[
                    ]ν   10   μ[
10   ]μει   τ.[
                   ]ọν̣φι   ρ[
                   ].υται   τ.[
                   ].ε̣ι̣α̣ν   ει.[
                    ]ν̣ọ[

                    .   .   .

Fr. 1 Col. i 1 An upright descending into l. 2 and turning out to right; perhaps a headless ρ
2 Perhaps υ but anomalously looped   3]., the end of a stroke from left touching c at mid letter;
α?   13]., the right-hand end of a cross-stroke touching the top of ε; τ not much suggested
    Col. ii 7 .[, an upright   8 .[, perhaps α   9 .[, a trace compatible with α, or possibly
with λ   11 .[, an upright with the foot hooked to right; possibly the left-hand stroke of ω
14 .[, a speck level with the top of the letters

Fr. 2   Fr. 3

```
            ·    ·                      ·        ·
          ]..[                        ].[
        ]αυτουϲυπ[                   ]λοιϲθ[
        ].τ[.]εφομεν[                ]ϲμετα[
      ].αλουϲ ενο[.]..ρο[            ] νε.[
  5   ]ναυτουϲπαρ[.].αλεικ[      5   ].ϲαν[
      ].εργαϲιαν αιτοκ.[             ·    ·    ·
      ].καιλεγεινηοτε‾ [
      ]θεοιϲιτ’ευχεϲθαι [
      ].ιπαντοϲηλογου[
 10   ]νοιτοθεοϲτιϲ...[
      ].ϲτιν   ϲτρ[
      ]τρ.τονοχ[
      ]εαιδελωμ[
      ].οιπροθυμ[
 15   ]νδιϲοιομ[
      ]..οϲοεξηϲλ[
      ]ϲθαοτεα[
      ]ν.[
            ·    ·    ·
```

Frr. 2 and **3** look as if they cannot have been far apart, but I cannot place them in any particular relation to one another

Fr. 2 1 The foot of a stroke descending well below the line, followed by the lower part of an upright 3]., the turn up of ε, ϲ suggested   4]., the right-hand end of a stroke, touching α at mid letter, and a dot below it below the line   ].., perhaps the overhang of ϲ touched by the tail of φ in l. 3; if so, followed by π   ο[remade by 1 m.   5]., one or two faint dots; no letter verifiable   6]., the lower end of a stroke descending from left, above which the right-hand end of a slightly domed stroke level with the top of the letters; κ, χ, or ϲ not suggested   For αιτο I am not sure that απο is not to be read   .[, a dot about mid letter   7]., an upright with a median trace to left   9]., the right-hand end of a cross-stroke touching ι, which is unusually tall, below its top   10 ...[, the top of ο or θ, the top of ε, the left-hand branch of υ or χ suggested   11]., the top and bottom of an upright   Of ρ[only the lower end of the stalk   12 Between ρ and τ presumably α intended, but not now to be made of the ink   14]., the right-hand end of a cross-stroke; ε suggested   15 δ apparently made out of ο by 1 m.   16]., the upper end of a stroke descending to right, followed by the right-hand side of a small loop level with the top of the letters

Fr. 3 4 .[, an upright   5]., the lower end of a stroke curving down from left

Fr. 2 3 ϲτ[ρ]εφομεν[suggested.
5 παρακαλει likely.

Fr. 4

.   .

].[

]εϲτι[ ]υτωϲιτρ..[

]ητετουκαρπου μ[

]ητεαμωντεϲο[

5   ].ωϲτρειακοντα[

]μ.ν[

.   .   .

Fr. 4 2 Of τι[only the lower parts ..[, a dot level with the top of the letters to right of which on the line the foot of a stroke hooked to right, followed by the lower part of an upright   3 υκ retouched by 1 m.   4 μ on π?, 1 m.   6 Tops of letters. Between μ and ν only one or two specks

Fr. 4 2 ο]ύτωϲί.

τρυ. seems unavoidable, but υ would be anomalously written. If υ, τρυγ[is a natural guess.

4 I should have thought that π was written on μ (not μ on π), but μ produces a series of letters of which it is easier to make something and apparently with some relevance to the preceding. ? μ]ήτε τοῦ καρποῦ. μ[ήτε ...... μ]ήτε ἀμῶντες.

Fr. 5

(a)   (b)

. . .   . . .

].αγαι.[   ].[

].[ ].ηνπαρ[   ]χαγα.[

]αϲ.υπ..ειαμμ[   ].ϲτυ.[α ϲτυπάζει Ἀμμ[ώνιος   ].ϲτυπ[

]παιε[]ξυλοκοπηϲω[   ]τονε..[παιε[] ξυλοκοπήϲω[   ]τονε..[

5]καιτ[.]παραρχιλοχω[   ].παρθε[καὶ τ[ὸ] παρ' Ἀρχιλόχω[ι   ]. παρθέ-

].οιθυρεωναπεϲτυ[   ]..χαιρι[νοι θυρέων ἀπεϲτύ[παζ   ]ον Χαῖρι[

.]τυπαζει ϲτυπ.ακ[   ]..ιλευκα[ϲ]τυπάζει ϲτυπιακ[   ]..ιλευκα[

]ωιπτιλλ.υτιθη.[   ]νταταιπ[   ]ωιπτιλλ.υτιθη.[   ]νταταιπ[

].ανκοραι·επλι[   ].νκ.[   ].αν κόραι· επλι[   ].νκ.[

10]ηνκυϲοδακνι.[   ].ενταυ [   ]ην κυϲοδακνια[   ]. ἐν ταυ-

]ωικατατοναυ....[   ]ντοιϲπρ[τ]ῶι κατὰ τὸν αὐτὸν .[   ]ν τοῖϲ πρ[ο-

]ρημενοιϲκ....[   ]νδιδω[ει]ρημένοις κ....[   ]ν δίδω-

]ναυτωικυϲοκνηϲ[   ]πρωκ.[ϲι]ν αὐτῶι κυϲοκνηϲ[ιᾶν   ]πρωκτ[

]ριανϊνηφ....του[   ]ου και[ψω]ριᾶν ἵν' ηφ....του[   ]ου και[

15]νκ.[].....[]ν ι[   ]θανατο[

                    ]ινπ[

. . .   . . .

Fr. 5 The relative levels of (*a*) and (*b*) are fixed by the cross-fibres. Their distance apart is not determinable by external evidence. The internal evidence of the text on the back (above) suggests an approximate but not a precise estimation of the interval. The text on the front provides no evidence since the gap falls in the blank space between columns

1]., prima facie the right-hand part of τ   .[, on the line a loop open to right   ].[, the feet of two uprights, perhaps separate letters   2].[, the lower part of an upright   ]., γ, τ, or even π, apparently possible   .[, the lower part of an upright   3 Above the first letters a dot on a single fibre in the interlinear space   ]., a dot on the line   Of ς only the turn-up and the tip of the overhang   4 ..[, the lower part of an upright with a dot on the line immediately to right, perhaps the base of c, followed by the foot of an upright   5]., a cross-stroke touching the left-hand angle of π; perhaps ε, but α not ruled out   6 Of]ο only the base;]α equally possible   7 Between π and ι a trace not accounted for, just above mid letter   ].., perhaps the right-hand ends of the overhang and of the cross-stroke of ε, followed by a small crescent, facing left, at mid letter, resembling the upper part of ξ, but much lower than ξ in l. 4   8 I am not sure whether or not a letter is lost between λ and υ   .[, a trace not quite level with the top of the letters   ται, there is a curved stroke over the tip of ι not accounted for   9]., an upright; I am not sure whether or not there is the right-hand end of an accompanying cross-stroke against the top of α   λι[, not prima facie αι[or ν[   ]., perhaps η, but anomalous. If]_υ, not]ου   10 Of α[only a trace of the apex   ]., a trace about mid letter 12 The count of letters is uncertain. After κ elements of an upright followed by a dot level with its top, then strokes resembling the lower part of the left-hand upright and the cross-stroke of η, then a triangular letter, δ or λ, followed by the lower part of an upright descending well below the line   14 Midway between φ and τ a crescent, open to right, on the line, followed by an upright; on either side of these scattered dots   Of τ only the cross-stroke   15 In the middle of the line the papyrus is broken off just below the tops of the letters, which are also otherwise damaged. The count is more or less a guess. Of ο[only the top left-hand arc; π might be an alternative to το[

Fr. 5 The closest estimate of the interval between (*a*) and (*b*) looks likely to be arrived at by postulating κατὰ τὸν αὐτὸν τ[όπο]ν or τ[ρόπο]ν (Hdt. i 5 with Stein's note) in l. 11. In that case -cτύ[παζ]ον, l. 6, and -c[ιαν]πρω-, l. 13, may be taken as about occupying the available space. As the facing edges of the two fragments are irregular, the establishment of these facts is most of the time of no practical importance.

3 α must be the first letter of the line. Unless it is a complete word, that is, ἆ or ἄ, which I should say was unlikely, it must have been preceded by a vowel.

Hesych. cτυπάζει· βροντᾶι, ψοφεῖ, ὠθεῖ.

Ἀμμ[ώνιος   ]. cτύπ[ει | παίε[ι]? Ammonius interprets bludgeons as hits with a stump.

Ἀμμ[ώνιοc and Χαῖρι[c, l. 6, may be considered to lend one another support. These two followers of Aristarchus are quoted in the scholia on Aristophanes. The piece on which the present commentary is written appears to be literature of a comparable kind.

The Χαῖριc of Aristophanes and other comic poets can hardly be considered here.

4 ξυλοκοπήcω: one of the senses of ξυλοκοπεῖν is 'beat with a club', though the lexicon gives no earlier sources for this meaning than Polybius and Arrian. I must suppose that ξυλοκοπήcω is adduced, presumably in a quotation, for the parallel in meaning. But I do not understand the abruptness of its appearance.

5 θυρέων ἀπεcτύπαζον is Archil. fr. 127, παρθένοι and what preceded is new.

6 seqq. I should guess, an interpretation of cτυπάζει offered by Chairis, followed by a quotation that goes as far as κόραι in l. 9. As the quotation, though I cannot in the least follow a thread of sense in it, seems at any rate irrelevant to words signifying 'beating', perhaps it is a lemma. If so, an Ionic author is ruled out by κόραι for κοῦραι.

10 Hesychius has κυcοδακνία· ψωρία, emended, since the noun is ψώρα, to -ιᾶι . . . -ιᾶι. This may be right, but other possibilities are easily thought of, so that I am uncertain whether I am right in accenting κυcοκνηcιᾶν . . . ψωριᾶν in ll. 13 seq. or whether the truth may not be κυcοκνηcίαν πρωκτο-ψωρίαν.

11 seq. 'in the same . . . as the aforesaid . . .'

14 ἵν᾽ ἦι? 'so that the sense is'.

2812. COMMENTARY ON A TRAGEDY?

Commentaries on poetical texts resemble each other very much in method and layout. Some are more liberal than others in their provision of means for distinguishing the lemmata (*paragraphi*, projecting lines, blank spaces, colons, or other signs) and the present specimen is in this respect extremely simple, using only the *paragraphus* and projecting line (n. on fr. 1 (*a*) ii 12). So far as I can judge it was neither diffuse nor rambling and some learning is evinced in the quotation of Dionysius, Nicander (?), and perhaps Alcman. Apollodorus was evidently not directly used.

What has been preserved of the text to which the commentary applies is in iambic trimeters of a sort which prima facie come from a tragedy. I can make no guess what tragedy. From what we are told in the upper part of fr. 1 (*a*) ii one may infer that there was a reference either to concerted action by Poseidon and Apollo, such as they took against Laomedon, or similar action, such as the one took against Laomedon, the other against Laocoon. But the reference may have been incidental. Certainly Laomedon and Laocoon cannot have occurred as principals in the same play.

One must take legends as one finds them but I cannot refrain from pointing out that great difficulties would be removed and the view I have propounded about the argument contained in ll. 16–36 much altered, if it were allowable to suppose that Laocoon (whose name is both times supplied) did not come into the question at all, but that what the commentator says is simply, that in the play (as in Nicander's version of the story) Laomedon was punished by Poseidon through the dispatch of a sea monster and by Apollo through the dispatch of sea-serpents, or rather, to speak more accurately, that there was something in the play which could be interpreted to mean that. But to suppose this requires the transference of an elaborately detailed and multifariously attested feature of the Laocoon story to Laomedon and I know of no evidence that would justify it.

The hand is a legible cursive without abbreviations which I should assign to the first century. The writer has corrected himself in two or three places; in l. 28 c of κολωνας seems to have been inserted by another pen. There are no lection signs. ⁒ against fr. 1 (*a*) ii 5 may call attention to the proper name. The purpose of the heavy dot against l. 37 does not appear.

Fr. 1 (*a*)

Col. i   Col. ii

```
      ]͵ητος              καιφοιβοϲαπολλων[
      ]ͺτην               αθληϲαντεο.[....].[
     ]νθει                ͵ενπο...δωναφηϲιν.[
      ]ͺϲαμεν             μεδοντιτοτειχοϲτονδ.[
5    ]τον            5 %  ͵αιδιονυϲιοϲγουναναλ[
     ]..μος              τωιφηϲινουτωϲμεταδε[
     ]ͺαιαλκμ̅ᵃ           μιμνηιϲκειαυτοντηϲαπ.[
     ]ριτουγα            τρωϲε̇ινοτεποϲειδωνοϲ.[
     ]υκηνθεν            ͵οτειχοϲπεριτροιαναπολλ[
10   ]ͺναφιοͺ[      10 ]  οιϲ[...]ϲτατηϲα[.]τοϲλαομͺ[
     ]ͺϲτρα[          ]  κα[...]ͺκεναυτο[ͺ]ϲτονμιͺ[
                        ]λη̲[ͺ]ͺαϲεξεβαλενκαιλογο.[
                        ]ριαϲουτωϲεπαληθειαϲαͺ[
                        ]ϲειδωνοϲλεγεταικαιθεμ[
                   15       ]ͺτεϲειϲμοιτουτωιπρ[
                        ]ολλω̈ννομιοϲενιοιδεκ.[
                        ]ηπτικωϲηκ[....]ͺωϲτεͺ[
                        ]οϲκαιεπιτ[..]ολλωνιϲυντετ[
                        ]ͺανδροϲεξειργαϲθαιανδοξειενͺ[
                   20   ]ϲτοριαντονμενγαρποϲειδωναͺ[
                        ]ωιλαομεδον[ͺ]ͺιτοκητοϲεπιπεͺ[
                        ]ολλωνατουϲͺͺεργαϲαμενουϲτ[
                        ]οϲυιονδρακονταϲγραφωνεντηι.[
                   ]  τοντροποντουτονιλοϲδαφραδιη[
                   25 ]  περιδωμεενατηϲοϲδηλαομεδο.[
                   ]  ρεκτηιλιπετιμηνοϲπρωτοϲψυθι[
                   ]  ληιϲϲατομυθου̇ϲευτεποϲειδαωͺ[
                        ]μαδαϲαμφικολωναϲλαινεονπͺ[
                        ]αρτυγατοͺͺρουφοιβοϲδι[
                   30 ]...[     ].[].[   ]ͺοͺ[
                   ]     ϲχεδε[ͺ]ηλαϲεκητοϲπανταδεͅη[
                   ]     καταχννεϲκεδελαουϲθηρειουδορͺ[
             ]ͺυ          λοϲπροκρινατοπαϲαϲαυταροθυμβρα[
       ].[.].[.].[.]ͺη   αλϲεͺθρεψεδρακονταϲποικηνͺͺ[
       ]τουͺ[ͺ].   35   ανοτεπρολιποντͺκαλυδναϲυιεͺ[
       ]ͺοπου[ͺ]ͺι        υπερͺωμωνεπαϲαντοοιαϲθεαϲεͺ[
       ]φαρουυ           ͺρωιͺͺλͺαφειτεμιϲειτουβοτηραρχ[
       ]ͺαιτην           ρωͺͺνκαταχρηϲειεφηαͷτιτουπ[
       ]ͺη..ουͨ[         ]το̲δεαφειτεαντιτουπροιεͅ[
       ]ͺαϲπο̣ [    40  ]ͺνδεͺονξυνηλιωιτωινͺͺ[
       ]φαρο̣υ          [.]τ[ͺͺ]νκυκλοϲηραϲαθαν[
       ]ͺιεβη           δοͺ[ͺ]ͺιμητοργιαϲταϲτο[
Fr. 1 (b)  ]ͺνυν         τουͺ[ͺͺ]ριζομαιορ̅οντιθεμ[
  ]ͺικͺ[                [ ]..[ͺͺͺ]ωϲανειελεγενθυϲιᾳ[
  ]ͺνμν[    ]..    45   ]ͷκυριωϲελεγοντοͺ[
  ]ͷιϲυμβ[              ]ͺιατοενταιϲαͷργαιϲ[
  ]ͷνηκτͺ[              ]ͺλειϲͺαιιϲωϲδεκα[
  ]ͺτοιϲπεͺ[            ]τεϲεντᾳͺ[
                        ]ρα̣[
```

καὶ Φοῖβος Ἀπόλλων [ἥρωι Λαομέδοντι πολίσσαμεν
ἀθλήσαντε. ο . [. . . .] . [τὸν
μὲν Ποσειδῶνά φησιν . [τῶι Λαομέδοντι τὸ τεῖχος τὸν δὲ [Ἀπόλλωνα   -
5   σαι. Διονύσιος γοῦν ἀναλ[-
τωι φησιν οὕτως· μετὰ δὲ[-
μιμνήισκει αὐτὸν τῆς ἀπ . [τοῖς
Τρῶσιν, ὅτε Ποσειδῶνος μ[ὲν
τὸ τεῖχος περὶ Τροίαν Ἀπόλλ[ωνος δὲ τοῖς ποιμνί-
10   οις [ἐπι]στατήσα[ν]τος Λαομέδων
κα[. . .] . κεν αὐτο[ῖ]ς τὸν μι[σθὸν   ἀπει-
λή[σ]ας ἐξέβαλεν. καὶ λόγου[
]ριας οὕτως ἐπ’ ἀληθείας α . [Ποσειδῶνος λέγεται καὶ θεμ[
15   . . . . ο]ἵ τε σεισμοὶ τούτωι πρ[ος-   ὁ δὲ Ἀ-
π]όλλων νόμιος. ἔνιοι δὲ κα[
λ]ηπτικῶς ἤκ[ουσα]ν ὥστε . [-
.]ος καὶ ἐπὶ τ[ἀπ]όλλωνι συντετ[-
. ανδρος ἐξειργάσθαι ἂν δόξειεν . [
20   ἱ]στορίαν. τὸν μὲν γὰρ Ποσειδῶνα . [
τ]ῶι Λαομέδον[τ]ι τὸ κῆτος ἐπιπέμ[ψαι τὸν δὲ Ἀ-
π]όλλωνα τοὺς διεργασαμένους τ[ὸν τοῦ Λαοκόων-
τ]ος υἱὸν δράκοντας, γράφων ἐν τῆι . [
τὸν τρόπον τοῦτον· Ἶλος δ’ ἀφραδί[ηισι λόφον
25   περιδώμεεν Ἄτης, ὃς δὴ Λαομέδον[τι κακορ-
ρέκτηι λίπε τιμήν, ὃς πρῶτος ψυθί[οισι θεοὺς
λήισσατο μύθοις, εὖτε Ποσειδάων[
μάδας ἀμφὶ κολωνάς λαΐνεον πυ[
κ]αρτύνατο χώρου Φοῖβος δ’ ι[
30   . . . [. . . . . .] . [. . .] . [. . . . . .] . ο . [
σχεδε[.] ἤλασε κῆτος πάντα δελη[
καταχνύεσκε δὲ λαούς θηρείου δορ . [
λος προκρίνατο πάσας, αὐτὰρ ὁ Θυμβρα[ῖος τοὺς
ἇλς ἔθρεψε δράκοντας, Πόρκην κα[ὶ Χαρίβοι-
35   αν, ὅτε προλιπόντε Καλύδνας υἱέ[α Λαοκόωντος
ὑπὲρ βωμῶν ἐπάσαντο. οἵας θεασε[
ρωι . . λ . ἀφεῖτε μίσει τοῦ βοτηραρχ[. . -
ρω . . ν καταχρήσει ἔφη ἀντὶ τοῦ π[
τὸ δὲ ἀφεῖτε ἀντὶ τοῦ προίε[τε.
40   ] . νδεσον ξὺν ἡλίωι τῶι νῦν[
[.]τ[. .]ν κύκλος ηρασαθαν[
δο . [.]τι μήτ’ ὀργιαστὰς το[
του[. ὁ]ρίζομαι ὅρον τίθεμ[αι   ὀργια-
ςτ[άς]ὡσανεὶ ἔλεγεν θυσια[στάς
45   ]ν κυρίως ἐλέγοντο ὀ[ργιασταί
δ]ιὰ τὸ ἐν ταῖς ὀργαῖς . [
τ]ελεῖσθαι. ἴσως δὲ κα[
]τες εντατ . [
]ρα[

Fr. 1 (*a*) Col. i is written slightly smaller than col. ii so that the end of i 11 stands level with ii 10   1]., the right-hand arc of a circle, o probable, but ρ not excluded   4]., the lower part of a stroke descending from left ligatured with ϲ, e.g. α, λ   6].., below the line the foot of an upright and of a stroke slanting up to right   7]., the end of a stroke ascending from the line to run into α, probably κ   10 Perhaps].ον should be written, the remains of the first letter being a stroke descending from left to right into the top of ρ   ο[rather small and high, ε[not ruled out   11]., perhaps the upper right-hand side of o   35 .[, a loop on the line, α one possibility. Another perhaps ν with no whole letter lost after it   ]., the upper right-hand arc of a circle off the line, perhaps o or ρ   36]αι possible, but the first letter is smudged   38]., a horizontal stroke from left touching the top of the loop of α   40]., the upper end of a stroke rising from left to touch the top of the loop of α   41 For ον perhaps αι   42]., a stroke descending from left through the lower part of ι   44].., perhaps a ligature followed by ρ

Fr. 1 (*b*) The level is fixed by cross-fibres. It seems to me probable that the scrap should be placed to left of fr. 1(*a*) col. i under the projecting lines, 34–8, so that no whole letter is lost between κ.[and].ν in l. 43

43].ι, perhaps a ligature   44]. traces of a stroke descending below the line   47 .[, a trace well below the line

Fr. 1 (*a*) Col. ii 2 .[, a stroke rising from the line with a curve to right, μ or ν probable   ].[, the foot of a stroke sloping slightly to right   3 .[, a loop below the line open to right   7 .[, the extreme left-hand lower arc of a circular letter   11]., a small circle off the line which suggests ρ more than any other letter   13 .[, the start of a curved stroke rising to right from the tail of α   19]., the tail of a stroke curving up into the back of α, e.g. κ, λ, μ   .[, the lower left-hand quarter of a circle   20 .[, a small loop on the line, φ possible   21 λαο made out of με by the original writer   23 .[, a short curved stroke, open to right, on the line   30 Before o either a single letter, e.g. π, or a letter ligatured with ι, e.g. ϲι, τι, among the possibilities. After o perhaps the start of μ or ν. πο*ν*[τ might be chosen for the sense   34 Between ε and θ a stroke level with the top of the letters. Perhaps the copyist started to write ετρεψε, but there is no visible sign of correction   35 Between τ and κ ε written on α by the original writer   37 After ωι the left-hand side and top of what I should have taken for o, if what seems to be an o did not follow. Perhaps therefore πο   At an interval after λ the lower end of a stroke below the line; if ι, there is room for a letter ligatured with it after λ, e.g. λ[ε]ι   38 Between ω and ν the lower tip of a stroke descending below the line and the top of an upright   40]., a dot level with the top of the letters   42 .[, the upper part of an upright slightly hooked to left at the top and curving to right at the lower end; ν would suit   [.], some two-letter combinations would stand   48 .[, the left-hand arc of a circle

Fr. 1 (*a*) Col. i 7 Alcman mentioned. ἦνθεν, l. 9, may denote a direct quotation from him. But there are other articulations.

8 In the context Γα][νυμήδουϲ is worth bearing in mind.

Col. ii The supplements of ll. 1, 21–2, 24–6, 33–5 show a variation in the number of letters to the line between 33 and 40.

1 seq. *Il.* vii 452 seq. In this place Apollo takes part in the building of the walls of Troy.

3 E.g. ἀ[περγάϲαϲθαι.

4 E.g. βουκολῆ|ϲαι.

5 seqq. The quotation from Dionysius appears to be not a comment on a text but a passage from a historical work in which legend is adduced to point a warning: 'thereupon he reminded him of the consequence to Troy of Laomedon's cheating Poseidon and Apollo of their wages.' Its interest for the writer of this commentary is no doubt that it contains a version of the story which confirms (γοῦν) the version referred to in 2 seqq., namely, that only Poseidon built the walls of Troy while Apollo tended Laomedon's herd. That is the version found in *Il.* xxi 446 seqq., but if Homer is the subject of φηϲιν, l. 3, it is odd that confirmation of his account by Dionysius should be offered.

10 seq. οὐκ ἀπέδωκεν would be expected and cannot be quite ruled out but]ω is not a satisfactory interpretation of the ink.

12 seq. At 36 seq. a fresh lemma starting in mid-line is marked by a *paragraphus* under the beginning of the line in which it starts and the projection of the following line into the left-hand margin. There is

therefore a presumption that a lemma starts in l. 12 (of which]ριac in l. 13 formed part if, which I think improbable, a letter projecting into the left-hand margin is lost before it), but this seems not to be so.

I strongly suspect that Ποcειδῶνοc is a mistake, and that it should be emended and 13 seqq. supplemented in the light of Schol. B on *Il.* xxi 447 ἀcφάλιος γὰρ καὶ θεμελιοῦχος ὁ Ποcειδῶν . . . ὁ δὲ Ἀπόλλων νόμιος . . . (cf. Schol. Gen. *ibid.*, a verbal quotation of Apollodorus, π. θεῶν). In that case there should perhaps be recognized in καὶ λόγον κτλ. the 'explanation' of their roles in the 'story' (ἱcτο|ρίαc?) by reference to their theological functions.

15 E.g. πρ[οcνέμονται.

16 seqq. I should guess this to be the comment on the lost text: 'some take' such and such a word or phrase (τ[ὸ "... | .]οc") 'inclusively (cυλ[λ]ηπτικῶc), construing it as applying to Apollo as well (as Poseidon)'. To judge from the quotation, 24 seqq. (resumed by the commentator, 20 seqq.), adduced in support of this interpretation (γάρ, l. 20), the reference is to the fact that both gods punished offenders by means of creatures sent against them out of the sea. But ἐπί with the genitive, not dative, would be commoner grammatical usage and the crasis τ[απ]ολλωνι is unexpected.

19 Νί|κανδροc is perhaps the likeliest of the possible names but there is nothing to guide us in assigning the verses to any of his known works possessing a suitable feminine title. Ε[ὐρωπ-, C[ικελίαι are equally consistent with the trace at the end of l. 23. Πεί|cανδροc might seem to be suggested by Macrob. V ii 4, Θέc|cανδροc by Serv. in *Aen.* ii 211, but cαv is not a possible reading here. ἐξειργάcθαι of the activity of an author, LSJ. in v. I 5, to which might be added : Porph. ap. Schol. B on *Il.* x 252 διορθοῦν καὶ ἐ.

20 E.g. φ[ηcι μηνίοντα.

24 ἀφραδίηιcι: φηcὶ . . . Ἑλλάνικος ἐν ᾱ Τρωικῶν ὅτι μαντευομένωι ἐν Πριήπωι τῆς Φρυγίας τῶι Ἴλωι ἔχρηcεν ὁ Πριηπηναῖος Ἀπόλλων μὴ κτίζειν τὸν λόφον τοῦτον. Ἄτης γὰρ αὐτὸν ἔφη εἶναι, Schol. Lycoph. *Alex.* 29.

25 περιδώμεεν: the compound hitherto unattested, the form wrongly evolved from δώμεον, etc., where ε regularly develops out of α before ο, ω. For parallels see Pfeiffer, Callimachus vol. I Addend. fr. 83, 3 (p. 501), Bühler, *Hermes* Einzelschr. 13 p. 161.

λόφον . . . Ἄτης: Ilium; cf. besides the passage quoted above the references in *Roscher* Ate (2) or Leutsch, *Paroem. gr.* ii 14 (n. ad Diog. i 85).

26 ψυθίοιcι not attested in the sense of 'false' and abnormally formed if from ψύθος = ψεῦδος. See Pf. ad Call. fr. 93, 1.

28 Nothing better than [μὲν Ἀγαμ|μάδαc occurs to me. This adjective is not attested and Ἀγαμ-μεύc (Steph. Byz. in Ἀγάμμεια) would lead one to postulate Ἀγαμμίc.

29 I should have expected something like λαΐνεον πύργοιc(ι) . . . καρτύνατο τεῖχος. χώρου presumably depends on a word meaning something like cτεφάνη or εἶλαρ.

The remainder of this line and the next should contain (1) the reason for Apollo's anger with Laocoon, (2) the statement that 'therefore Poseidon (μέν)' etc., parallel to αὐτὰρ ὁ Θ. But the space is short.

30 seq. Presumably ἐπι preceded ἤλαcε. 'Neptunus iratus Troiae inmisit cetos quod eam uastaret', Serv. in *Aeneid.* i 550.

ἀcχαδέc is quoted from Aeschylus (fr. 418) as meaning ἀμετάcχετον or ἀκατάcτατον. If ἀκατάcχετον is meant, ἀcχεδέc might be the true form both there and here.

32 ἀχνύειν unattested; ἀχνύc Anon. ap. *Et. Mag.* 182, 3, ἀχνυόειc prob. Hdt. v 77 (A. Pal. VI 343). The general tenor of this line and those which precede and follow it must be gathered from Diod. iv 42, Schol. *Il.* xx 146, Schol. Lycophr. *Alex.* 472, 952, etc. I can make no satisfactory guess how it was expressed in detail. If -λοc is πά|λοc, I should have expected παcέων not πάcαc (cf. Diod. iv 42, 3 ἁπάν-των [sc. τέκνων] εἰς τὸν κλῆρον ἐμβαινόντων ἐπανελθεῖν εἰς Ἡcιόνην τὴν τοῦ βαcιλέωc θυγατέρα), but in that case there would scarcely be room for the object of the verb. If θηρείου δόρπου (-οιο), corresponding to βορὰν τῶι κήτει in Diodorus and the *Iliad* scholion, is the beginning of this verse, there is again no room for anything which would make the genitive comprehensible. I cannot avoid concluding that something is missing between λαούc and θηρείου.

33 ὁ Θυμβραῖος sc. ἐπήλαcε. Laocoon was the priest of Thymbraean Apollo (Serv. in *Aen.* ii 201), his sin was committed in the temple of Thymbraean Apollo (*ibid.*), his son was eaten there (Schol. Lycoph. *Alexandr.* 347). Euphorion also told or referred to the story, according to Servius l.c.

34 The names of the snakes appear in Schol. Lycoph. l.c. as Πόρκις and Χαρίβοια. Πόρκις is confirmed against Πόρκης by the genitive Πόρκεως (like ἔχις, ἔχεως) in Lycophron's text. I may, therefore, very well be wrong in correcting ποικην to πορκην instead of πορκιν. ποικην may have arisen from πορκὴν mistaken as πορκην. In Serv. in *Aen.* ii 211 the names are given as 'curifin et periboeam'. Sophocles is said (*ibid.* 204) to have mentioned them in his Λαοκόων but we are not told what form they had there.

35 υἱέα cf. τὸν . . . υἱόν 22 seq. In the 'Ιλίου πέρcιc of Arctinus one son and the father are killed, in Schol. Lycoph. l.c. one son, the father not being mentioned; in other versions both sons, with and without the father.

36 seq., 39 seqq. contain lemmata of the text on which the commentary is written. These lemmata are in iambic trimeters and prima facie come from a tragedy. There is something for and nothing against the possibility that the play may have had 'matter of Troy' for its subject, but I do not recognize anything to support an attempt to fix it more exactly or identify the author.

36 θεαcε[: various articulations open, θεαcε[from θεῶμαι, θεαc ἐ[from θέα or θεά, θεα cε[.

37 I should suppose that the word containing the syllable ρωι is the same word as that at the beginning of the next line, ρω‚.‚ν, since besides having the common syllable they both times stand in about the same position relatively to ἀφεῖτε. In that case in l. 37 read -ρωι ‚.‚λ. (possibly πόλ[ε]ι) and in l. 38 -ρωι ἐν, though ε is not strongly suggested by the traces and I find no example of ἐν καταχρήcει for καταχρηcτικῶc, although ἐκ κ. is not uncommon.

τοῦ βοτηραρχ[: it is easy to devise a sentence in which τοῦ would be the relative and βοτὴρ ἀρχ[thus articulated. But it seems to me not improbable that an unattested βοτηράρχης should be recognized.

41 ηραcαθαν[: various articulations open, some of no great probability. I will only call attention to the possibility of ἡράcαθ' (when κύκλοc might be 'people standing round'), and the impossibility of ἀθανατ-, which has a long first a.

42 δο‚.[‚.‚]τι: prima facie δου[‚.‚]τι, but I do not see how this is to be accommodated to the required trimeter ending. Some ligatured combinations of two letters take no more room than one but I find nothing very plausible.

44 seqq. Again I suspect error in the text. ἀργαιc, I believe, should be emended and the lines filled up in the light of *Et. Mag.* ὄργια· τὰ μυcτήρια· κυρίωc δὲ τὰ Διονυcιακὰ διὰ τὸ ἐν ταῖc ὀργάcιν αὐτοῦ (*leg.* αὐτὰ) ἐπιτελεῖcθαι.

Fr. 2   Fr. 3

```
        ·        ·                                    ·      ·     ·
     ].δη.[                                             ].νο[
    ]λημ[                                             ]εcημ[
      ]ημ[                                            ]cυμο.[
    ].παχ[
5    ].[.]ου[                                          ·      ·     ·
```

        ·   ·

Fr. 3 1]., the first letter perhaps intended for λ, but anomalous   2 Or possibly]α   3 .[, the left-hand arc of a circle

Fr. 2 1]., the lower part of an upright curving slightly to left at the top   .[, a horizontal stroke level with the top of the letters   4]., a short arc of the upper right-hand side of a circle   5].[, a stroke off the line curving down from left to right, perhaps δ

2813. Commentary on Eupolis, *Προϲπάλτιοι*

Very little is known about this play of Eupolis (even if PSI 1213 is rightly included in the remains) and the present commentary adds nothing but a few short lemmata. If the upper part of fr. 1 contains a summary account of the contents, I cannot tell from it what they were, except that the repetition of ἥρωεϲ (fr. 5) at some distance from the previous mention (fr. 1) might indicate a subject taking up a certain amount of room.

The writing, which becomes thicker as it proceeds, is in a professional hand, I suppose of the late second or third century, employing a small number of cursive forms, ligatures, and contractions. These increase the ambiguities normally associated with the interpretation of incompletely preserved letters. Some of the fragments recovered are so worm-eaten that it is useless to attempt to transcribe what is now left of the text.

Fr. 1

Col. i   Col. ii

(a)   .   (d)]ως . . [   ]ανην προ   γαζει   [
        ] . δη α . [   ]απεϲταληϲαν δεη   ηκωμωδι[
        ] . . ηγορε[   ] . προϲαυτουνέ   βανειναυ[
    ]χ[ ]μρυγραφ[   ]κωμωδιαν'. ταυτα   μους η ο[
5   ]αυτοντο . [   ] . ινβιαϲαμοι η   5   δομοντρ[
        ] . μτουϲπ . . [   ] . ταϲμηγραφειν   ταϲοψειϲ[
        ] . ωαϲδι . [   ]προ[. . .]ωνπαλι   πειωνμη[
        ]οϲαυτ . . ϲα[   ] . οτ[   ]τουϲηρωαϲ   τοαθλορ[
        ] . 'τπολειτε . αϲ[   ]π . οϲφυωϲ   βοοϲτικο[
10] . πωραδ . αγα[   ]οιπρεϲβειϲ   10   εντοιϲκακ . [
        ] . μ[ ]ο . [ ] . [   ]ϲ   περιταδε[
    ] . [] . [] . . . δ . . . [ ] . [. [.] . κατ . [
    ] . εχθη χοροϲδπ . [   ]ωφω[   ]θαικ . [
    ]ραιειδηχθηι . [   ]αλτιω . [   ]δημ . [
15] . ι . ευπολιδοϲ[   ]αιμ́υπ . [15   ]λομα[
        ] . θυϲ . [   ]αμα   [   ]αλειν[
                                  ]ϲθαιεκ . [   ]κουει . [
                                  ]ιδ'ευπολ[[   ]μοϲ[
    ]φα[. .]υϲ[   ]ϲδενιοι   εφυγ . δ' . [
        ] . δ'π . [(c)]λυφανου .   20   βουλευειν[
20] . . [|] . . [(b)   ]νεϲθαι   κιθαρωδοϲ[
        ] . ερον[   ]λ[ ] . [ ] . ϲθηναι   κμετοικ . [
        ] . ωμ[   ] . αϲ[] . [ ]νγ   ξενονκπρο[
        ] . ϲπ[   ]ναγ[   ]οιϲακρο   ϲταταιϲεχ[
        ]και[   ]υδο[   ]γελωτ'   25   πολειτηϲ . [
25]γελωτ . [   ]ιμην   ϲτατου ϲπ[
        ]φειδε[   ] . οϲ   κουϲιμοικρ[
                                  ] . εαπο   τηϲγηϲμαχθο[
                                  ] . ηθη   χθοϲμεπεικα . [
                                  ]νπ . [ ] .   30   κουφοτηϲδ'επει . [
30   ] . αϲω   αλλακουφοικφ[
                                  ] . . αιπροε   ϲυρακόϲιονη . [
                              ]δενι γελοιωϲ   ειην___τουτουϲ[
                              ]τιηρωτηϲεμε   ]   τιϲεξηκεϲτον . [
                          ]μηδενι[.]ιπειν οτιεϲ[   ]   ταλουκομιζω . [
35   ]' . ϲ . οϲκωμωδια[35   ]   π'γενομοντ́αυ[
                          ] . . [.]ϲτονχδιδαϲκει [ ]   νεινδοκειμ . . [
                          ] . . . . κοφαν . ι / δ'[   ]   μηδ'ύθλει μηφ[
                          ] . κ . οιον αποβελιϲκου[   ]   πειακλ̀ωγμοϲ . [
                          ] . η θ . ρμ[.] . ουμη[   ]   θρωπωνγ[
40   ]ϲεπει [40   ]   γλωτ τηϲ[
                                                      ]   τραγικοϲη[
                                                      .]δ . . παδ[

Fr. 1 Col. i The levels of (*a*), (*b*), (*c*) relatively to (*d*) are fixed by cross-fibres. There is no external evidence about the distance of (*a*) from (*d*) or the distance of (*b*) from (*c*) and (*c*) from (*d*); there appears to be some internal evidence to fix the distance of (*a*) from (*d*) within a fairly close approximation

I cannot follow the vertical fibres of (*a*) down into (*b*) with any confidence, but the position of (*b*) shown is not apparently incompatible with them. I believe it probable that (*c*) lies between (*a*) and (*d*), but have no positive evidence to offer

1 . . [, perhaps simply π, the left-hand upright retouched   2]., the lower part and the upper tip of a stroke rising to right; ? ⁄ i.e. (εcτι)   Above η the left-hand end of a cross-stroke, possibly belonging to the previous line   .[, a speck on the line   Above]α a cross-stroke rising towards its right-hand end   3]., a speck level with the top of the letters   .η, I should have *read* ει; before η is a sign like a reversed comma   ]., the upper part of an upright   4 Between ν and τ a cusp on the line; if, as I suppose, κ, the upper part completely erased   ταυτα converted from τοτα, below the ο of which the left-hand end of a cross-stroke   5]., not prima facie ε; if the right-hand part of μ, a dot above it unaccounted for   6]., the top of a circle   . . [, touching the turn-up of π a small loop open to right, followed by a dot well below the line on a single fibre   ]., prima facie ει, but perhaps .η. See comm.   7]., the extreme lower end of a stroke descending well below the line   .[, two dots close together followed by confused traces; perhaps ω   8 Between τ and c only traces; I should guess ου not οι   ]., a dot level with the top of the letters   Of ρ only the top, of τ[only the left-hand end of the cross-bar   Of]τ only the right-hand end of the cross-bar   9]., level with the top of the letters what looks like the turn-up of a stroke descending from left with a dot close below it. The sign like an exaggerated apostrophe appears to mean nothing different from the simple sloping stroke, see l. 37   10]., the right-hand end of a cross-stroke, level with the top of the letters, having a speck close to right; perhaps two letters represented   Ink descending below the line from the right-hand base angle of δ; between δ and α a heavy dot at mid letter   12].[].[]., converging strokes, e.g. the lower parts of χ, followed by traces on the line   Then the lower parts of cιδλοι seem compatible with the remains   ].[, ? the top of the loop of ρ   13]., the upper part of an upright   .[, at mid letter the lower end of a stroke rising to right   ω.[, a dot under the right-hand part of ω   14 .[, level with the top of the letters the top of a stroke hooked to left   15]., if ε, anomalous Before ε the top of an upright   16]., the upper part of an upright   θ small and perhaps ο intended   Of ς only the cross-stroke, but γ less likely   .[, a dot well below the line under the tail of κ   17 The sign between δ and ε presumably (ε), not an apostrophe   18 Of]ς only the extension of the cross-stroke   19]., the right-hand side of a small circle   .[, the upper left-hand arc of a circle?   -υ., the start of a stroke rising to right   20 (*a*)]. . [above the line the right-hand end of a stroke from left, followed by a cross-stroke, level with the top of the letters, having a stroke returning to left from the right-hand end; perhaps π, ζ, or ξ   (*b*)]. . [, the upper part of a stroke rising to right, followed by the lower part of a stroke curving down to left   (*c*)].[, the base of a circle   21]., the middle of a stroke descending from left, followed by the top of a stroke ascending from left to touch the tip of the upper part of an upright; not μ, perhaps two letters represented   ]., the end of a cross-stroke touching c near the top   22 (*b*)]., a speck on the line   (*c*)]., traces compatible with the loop of ρ   ].[, below the line the start of a stroke rising to right?   (*d*) Of]ν only the upper part of the right-hand arm   23]., an upright   25 .[, a dot below the level of the cross-stroke of τ   26]., a cross-stroke with a nick towards its right-hand end touching ο near the top; perhaps two letters represented   27]., perhaps μ   28].., I think .ι, say ει, likelier than a single ν   29 Of ρτ only the lower parts   .[]., the lower part of an upright descending into l. 30 e.g. ρ, followed after a break by a speck on the line   30]., a short forward-sloping stroke   31]., on the line the base of a small circle, followed by the foot of an upright; perhaps two letters, .τ   34 Of]μ only the right-hand apex   Of]ε only the tip   35]'., a dot level with the top of the letters Before ς, of which only the extended cross-stroke, two specks level with the top of the letters, at an interval after ς a short cross-stroke level with the top of the letters and a slightly arched shorter cross-stroke below it on the line   36 Of]ς only the extended cross-stroke   37]. . ., a slightly arched cross-stroke level with the top of the letters having a speck on the line below its right-hand end, followed by the middle of an upright, and this by a dot level with the top of the letters; perhaps only two letters represented   Before κ prima facie a short-tailed ρ having lost the top curve of its loop   After ν the lower part of an upright, followed by a dot on the line with a dot vertically above and the lower

part of an upright   38]., the lower end of a stroke curving down from left   Between κ and o too much ink for a single letter; δ, λ, and υ all fail to account completely for it   39]., a cross-stroke level with the top of the letters   Between θ and ρ a dot level with the top of the letters   ]., the extreme right-hand tips of two strokes close together level with the top of the letters

Fr. 1 Col. ii 2 Of δ_ι[only the left-hand base angle of δ and the lower end of ι   9 seq. There is an interlinear dot in the right-hand edge which I suppose represents a letter of l. 9   12 .[.]., the left-hand end and the right-hand end of cross-strokes level with the top of the letters   .[, the loop of α likely, but o not ruled out   13 .[, a slightly convex upright   14 .[, the lower left-hand arc of a circle   17 Of]κ only the right-hand ends of the branches   .[, a dot on the line   19 Between γ and δ presumably ε, but anomalous   .[, a stroke rising to right from below the line   22 .[, I think ε or η likelier than o or ω   25 .[, the upper left-hand arc of a circle?   29 .[, perhaps the start of the left-hand stroke of μ   32 .[, the start of a stroke rising to right; λ or μ suggested 34 .[, two dots, one median, the other vertically under it below the line   35 ζ retouched   .[, an upright   37 ..[, scattered dots; possibly o.[38 Of φ[only the end of the tail   39 .[, a forward-sloping stroke; not (εcτι)   43 After δ perhaps ει or .η

Fr. 1 Col. i What with the disjointed state of preservation and the many uncertainties of decipherment, I do not find anything to contribute to the understanding of this column but the following desultory observations.

The upper lines do not appear to contain lemmata, but to be by way of introduction or hypothesis to the comedy to which they are prefixed. How far this preliminary matter extends I cannot tell, but by l. 24 I believe that the occurrence of γελωτ' . . . γελωτ. may be taken to imply that the commentary has begun.

2 δ' is the usual representation of δέ in this manuscript. Perhaps, therefore, δεη is to be taken as part of a word beginning like δεηcόμενοι.

3 -ηγορε[Of the available compounds δη]μηγορε[looks to me the only one at all reconcilable with the ink. Compare the μ in (a) 6.

I think]. πρὸc αὐτοῦ. 'Him' sc. Eupolis, whose name is recognizable at ll. 15, 17.

3 seq. It is uncertain how much of the column is lost on the left. If νέον ἀρ]χ[ο]μ(έν)ου γράφ[ειν] κωμωδίαν, 'at the very beginning of his career as a writer of comedy', is correct and entire, it establishes the width of the column (at about 30 letters) and at the same time the interval between (a) and (d).

4 Apparently κ(αὶ) τὸ τὰ . . . corrected to κ(αὶ) ταυτα, of which both analysis and translation are ambiguous, ταῦτα or ταὐτά, 'these things' or 'at that'.

5 αὐτ(ῶν).

I suppose]ειν is likely, as an infinitive after βιαcάμ(εν)οι, though anomalous as a decipherment.

6]ομ(εν). The first person plural looks out of place.]o, the end of a neuter, μὲν . . ., perhaps more acceptable.

I am unable to decide between ποιήταc, which I think the likelier for sense, and πολείταc, which I should prefer as an interpretation of the remains and spacing.

7]ρωαc suitable as a decipherment, and ἥρωαc consonant with]τουc ἥρωαc, l. 8. Another reference to ἥρωεc (how they are depicted) at fr. 5, 22.

9 I suspect, simply δ(έ), what I have described being the right-hand base angle of a loosely made δ, and the apostrophe-like sign (which sometimes is used for ηc) meaning no more than the 'acute'-like stroke used in most other instances.

τ(ῶν) πολ{ε}ιτ(ῶν).

Probably ἑκαc[τ- and no doubt προcφυῶc, but neither verifiable.

13 η]νέχθη?

13 seq. Though I should not have supposed that what I have described represented ων[, I do not doubt that χορὸc δὲ Πρ[οcπ]αλτίων is to be recognized.

The specification of the chorus in the hypotheses of both tragedy and comedy commonly belongs to one of two types: ὁ χορὸc cυνέcτηκεν ἐξ . . . or -ντεc -νται ἐν χοροῦ cχήματι. Both admit of a certain amount of variation and in addition there are a few examples of forms belonging to neither. Two of these, παραγίνεται δὲ χορὸc Cαλαμινίων ναυτῶν, Soph. *Aj.*, and ὁ δὲ χορὸc ἐκ Θηβαίων ἐcτὶ παρθένων Aesch. *Sept.*, suggest the possibility of something like χορὸc δὲ Προcπαλτίων | παραγίνεται ἀνδ]ρ(ῶν).

The Προςπάλτιοι of Eupolis is quoted about half a dozen times. *Et. Mag.* in Δρυαχαρνεῦ (*Et. Gen.*) records that Prospaltians were made game of ὡς δικαςτικοί.

14 There is no doubt about the reading αιει δ(ε) ηχθηι. I can suggest neither translation nor correction.

18 -]φα[νο]υς to be remembered.

19 δ(ια).

-λυφανου.. The last letter can hardly have been ς, but even if it were, only two adjectives ending in -λυφανής would be added to the three nouns in -λύφανο- as possibilities for this place. None of these words seems to me worth considering. Nor does the theoretically available articulation -λυ φανοῦν -ται or φανουμ. I have nothing to suggest.

22 seq. ς]υγ-γ or κ?

24 seq. γελωτ' . . . γελωτ. may well represent lemma and comment.

32 seqq. εἰπεῖν μη]δενί . . . μηδενὶ [ε]ἰπεῖν.

32 γελοίως. 'The poet is making a joke' cf. schol. Aristoph. *Av.* 1297; 1614.

37 It is difficult to believe that some form of ςυκοφαντ-ειν, -ης, -ια, is not to be recognized, but υ is hardly admissible as a decipherment of the ink before κ and I can recognize no letter after τ. (ἔςτι) δ(έ).

38 I see nothing else as likely as κλοιόν (for which the Attic form is said to be κλῳόν, schol. Aristoph. *Vesp.* 897), a sort of collar or cangue, referred to by Eupolis in the Κόλακες (fr. 159, 16). The sign, which I then suppose to be a 'hyphen', is unusually deeply curved.

39 θερμ[]. ?

Col. ii 1 The spacing throughout does not seem to have any significance. But the blank after γαζει is much greater than any other and presumably has a purpose, I cannot suggest what.

2 seq. λαμ|βάνειν.

3 seqq. -μ(εν)ους . . . -δομ(εν)ον.

19 ἔφυγε δ(ια).[.

22 seqq. μετοικ- suggests προςτάταις at 23 seq. and προςτάτου at 25 seq.; v. e.g. Bekker *Anecd.* i 201 ἡρεῖτο . . . ἕκαςτος αὐτῶν (sc. τῶν μετοίκων) ὃν ἤθελε τῶν πολιτῶν τινα προςτάτην, Harpocr. in ἀπροςταςίου.

ξενον κ(αὶ) προ[might represent πρόξενον καὶ προςτάτην; cf. Aristoph. *Thesm.* 602 ὦ πρόξενε, schol. ὦ πρόςτατα (ibid. 576 προξενῶ schol. προΐςταμαι).

-ςταταιςεχ[ρ- may be illustrated by *Eccles.* 176 προςτάταις χρωμένην, Demosth. iii 27 χρωμένοις οἷς εἶπον προςτάταις, though these phrases do not relate to μέτοικοι.

28 seqq. τῆς γῆς μ(ὲν) ἄχθο[ς . . . ἄ]χθος μ(ὲν) ἐπεὶ . . . κουφότης δ(ὲ) ἐπεὶ . . .

The commentary appears to relate to a lemma containing the words γῆς ἄχθος, applied, I suppose, as elsewhere, to persons who are not pulling their weight (Plat. *Theaet.* 176 d, cf. *Il.* xviii 104, *Od.* xx 379), and the word κουφότης[1] applied to the same persons on account of a contrasting fault, say, as being lightweights (κοῦφοι κ(αὶ) φ[).

32 Cυρακόςιον here I suppose likely to be, not Syracusan, but Syracosius, an orator attacked with more or less violence by Aristophanes (*Av.* 1297), Eupolis (Πόλεις, fr. 207), and Phrynichus (Μονότροπος, fr. 26). δοκεῖ δὲ καὶ ψήφιςμα τεθεικέναι μὴ κωμωιδεῖςθαι ὀνομαςτί τινα schol. *Av.* l.c.

34 Ἐξήκεςτος. A Syracusan of this name is mentioned by Thucydides (vi 73). There is no likelihood that he would be mentioned by an Attic comedian.

Ἐξήκεςτος is explained in Hesychius as ἡταιρηκώς. ὅθεν τοὺς πρωκτοὺς ὁμωνύμως Ἐξηκέςτους ἔλεγον.

Ἐξηκεςτίδης is a quite distinct name, but since an Ἐξηκεςτίδης κωμωιδεῖται ὡς ξένος (schol. Aristoph. *Av.* 11) and the same or another is recorded as a κιθαρωιδός (ibid.), see 21–6 above.

36 π(αρα)γενόμ(εν)ον.

38 μηδ' ὕθλει μὴ φ[λυάρει, cf. schol. Aristoph. *Nub.* 783.

39 κλωγμός Eustath. 1504, 29 κλωγμὸς κατὰ τοὺς παλαιοὺς ἐν θεάτρωι διὰ ςτόματος πρὸς τὸν οὐρανίςκον ἀποτελούμενός φαςι ψόφος; Harpocr. in ἐκλώζετε· κλωςμὸν ἔλεγον τὸν γιγνόμενον ἐν τοῖς ςτόμαςι ψόφον, ὧι πρὸς τὰς ἐκβολὰς ἐχρῶντο τῶν ἀκροαμάτων ὧν οὐχ ἡδέως ἤκουον. The word occurs in a mysterious passage of Cratinus Πλοῦτοι (PSI 1212 fr. *a* 15), where prima facie it has another meaning.

39 seq. ἀν]θρώπων.

---

[1] Accented κουφότης, in our notation κουφοτής, said to be Attic in Arcad. π. τον. 28, Choerob. Καν. 326, 12.

Fr. 2

```
                ·           ·
        ].εντοιϲε[
       ]τοϊερειον[]τ.[
        ].λύν.[].οτ[
       ]ωμωδ....[
   5   ]πϙϙντεγ.[
       ]ερματạ.[
       ]ν οεδ αδ[
          ]..[
            ·      ·      ·
```

Fr. 2 Perhaps from the neighbourhood of fr. 1 col. i

1]., the right-hand end of a cross-stroke as of ϲ, τ   2 .[, the lower left-hand side of a circle 3]., if one letter, ω, but two, e.g.].ο, may be represented   To left of λ ink not accounted for   Of υ only the upper end of the right-hand branch; I am not sure that the ´ is not simply an extension of it .[, a slightly backward-sloping upright, ? υ   ]., the right-hand end of a cross-stroke touching the top of ο   4 Attached to δ perhaps a short arc of the top left-hand side of a circle   ..[, the lower part of a stroke descending from left, followed by the left-hand side of a circle   5 Of τ the right-hand end of the cross-stroke and the foot of the right-hand stroke   .[, the upper part of a stroke curving down to right   8 .[, the apex of a triangular letter

Fr. 2 4 κ]ωμωδ-.
5 τ(ων).

Fr. 3   Fr. 4

```
     ·    ·    ·                            ·    ·    ·
    ] [                                    ]..[
    ].κ[                                   ]ερωνν[
     ]νκ[                                  ].πορευ.[
    ]αιδ.[                                 ].ειμιạ.[
    ].δον[                            5   ].ωιεθει.[
5   ]αυπ[                                  ].[
     ·    ·    ·                            ·    ·    ·
```

Fr. 3 1]., the upper end of a stroke rising from left to touch the upright of κ below the top 2 Of]ν only the top right-hand angle 3 .[, the lower end of a stroke descending below the line 4]., on the line the end of a stroke rising from left 5]α anomalous, perhaps through damage

Fr. 4 1 Now resemble α followed by a comma 3]., a cross-stroke touching the left-hand angle of π   .[, the left-hand arc of a circle 4]., the right-hand arc of a circle   .[, the start of a stroke rising to right 5]., the upper part of an upright ligatured to ω; not π   .[, perhaps the left-hand base angle of δ 6 The upper part of a stroke rising from left with a dot above

Fr. 5

```
          ]....[
          ]νασσχ[
          ]εικτο.[
          ]ρυκρειϙ[
   5      ]δ'οτιτι.[
          ].οιδ'οτιπ[
          ]εχθρανπα[
          ]ωβοσκεις [
          ]ωμωδειθ.[
  10      ]ξεδ'ινακακωσκρ[
          ]νωσφρυγα μαδι.[
          ].ευανδρου τουα[
          ]ς ματερμεγαλα [
          ]εσαυλ−ηταιενταις[
  15      ]χομοιανακρουες[
          ]θειξυμμαιν.[
          ]ρϙ.[  ]νφαυλον.[].. ϙ.[
          ].υ.[  ]φλαυρϙγκακον[
          ].[  ]επιπονον ὄῡγ'ε[
  20      ].κρατης τοιχωρυχο[
          ]υσινενδονμετοφεω[
          ]ηρωεςζωγραφουνται..[
          ]ες καπικήκαστον ε[
          ]βοιαπροιτουτουκορι[
  25      ].αυτλεγειουτοσς[
          ].[  ]νοντα αρ.[
          ].. κ.φι.[
          ]...[
          ]..αι.[
```

· · ·

Fr. 5 3 .[, a small loop open to right   5 .[, the foot of a forward-sloping stroke with a trace to right   6]., the upper part of a stroke rising from left   10 Between κρ a dot not accounted for   12]., perhaps ϲ, represented by the right-hand ends of its upper and lower parts   14 Of γ only the extreme bottom of the stalk   ταιϲ ex τοιϲ   16 .[, a tall upright with top hooked over to left   17 Rubbed   .[, the foot of an upright close to ϙ   .[, the lower part of an upright   ].., the lower part of an upright descending below the line, followed by the start of a stroke rising to right   .[, a dot on the line, followed by a loop open to right; perhaps two letters   18]., the upper right-hand arc of a small circle   .[, perhaps β likeliest, but anomalous   κα, the loop of α remade   19].[, the tail of a stroke descending into l. 20   20]., a dot on the line   22 ..[, prima facie, the loop of α having be ow it the left-hand end of the tail of a longtailed letter   25]., an upright; ν acceptable 26 .[, a concave upright   27].., what remains suggests αρ, but I believe this illusory, particularly as ρ has no tail   Between κ and φ what now looks like a small *diple* sprouting from the arms of κ, followed by a thick dot on the line

Fr. 5 3 κ(αί).

4 εὐ]ρυκρειο[ν presumably in a quotation or parody. κρείων Διομήδης Cratinus in Εὐνεῖδαι (fr. 68). 5 seq. Perhaps εὖ οἶ]δ' ὅτι . . . ε]ὖ οἶδ' ὅτι . . .

9 κ]ωμωιδεῖ.

11 Φρύγα perhaps an indication that Μεγάλη Μήτηρ is here thought of as the Phrygian goddess Cybele.

μὰ Δί'.[

12 If Εὐάνδρου (with or without τοῦ Ἀ[ρκάδος), possibly a reference to the figure in the proverb Εὔανδρος εὗρε (sc. κνημῖδα καὶ ἀσπίδα, Apostol. viii 14a), but εὔανδρον γᾶν Κέκροπος, Attica, Aristoph. *Nub.* 300.

13 Μᾶτερ μεγάλα, a quotation, or parody, or a non-Attic character speaking.

14 seq. αὐληταὶ . . . [ἀρ]χόμ(εν)οι ἀνακρούες[θαι: 'striking up, beginning a tune'.

17 seqq. The presence in the same neighbourhood of φαῦλον, φλαῦρον, κακόν, on the one hand, and ἐπίπονον, on the other, suggests the possibility of a play on πονηρός, like that in Epicharm. Ὀδ. αὐτομ. at **2429** fr. 1 ii 13.

20 It may be worth mentioning that the father of Orestes the footpad was called Timocrates, schol. Aristoph. *Av.* 1487. (Lysicrates *Av.* 513, though κλέπτης τε καὶ πανοῦργος, seems to have been of a higher social class than a τοιχώρυχος.)

τοιχώρυχο[ς ὁ -κράτης (cf. schol. Aristoph. *Av.* 988) or something of the sort.

21 -ο]υσιν ἔνδον μετ' ὀφέω[ν.

22 οἱ] ἥρωες ζωγραφοῦνται: 'are depicted'—with serpents? as serpents? The two doubtful letters seem to be αι[or αρ[or possibly αφ[, but not οφ[.

23 ἐπικήκαστον· τὸ ἐπονείδιστον καὶ καταγέλαστον Eustath. 1402, 53.

24 Cθενέ]βοια Προίτου τοῦ —. Stheneboia was the wife of Proetus, but Proetus was not a Corinthian. The mistake[1] (if there was a mistake) of Κορι[νθίου for Τιρυνθίου may be explicable by the fact that a Corinthian plays a part in the story, Bellerophontes alluded to in Euripides Cθενέβοια (fr. 664) and by way of parody in Aristophanes Θεcμοφοριάζουcαι 404 in the words τῶι Κορινθίωι ξένωι (cf. Cratin. fr. 273). But it should be said that it is possible—I do not think it is likely—that what stood here was something of the form of 'S., of P., who did something in regard to the Corinthian, wife'.

25 αὐτ(ήν).

Fr. 6

]ερ[

destroyed

] κια.[

] προο[

5   ]   [

   ]   κν[

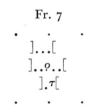

Fr. 7

]...[

].ο..[

].τ[

Fr. 6 3 .[, on the line a loop open to right 4 I cannot rule out ς[

Fr. 7 1]., the bottom right-hand arc of a circle? ..[, two converging strokes (not λ or χ), followed by a short flat stroke on the line 2]., perhaps α, ε, or ς, followed by ι ..[, a short upright off the line, followed by a short flat stroke on the line 3]., the top of an upright? Over τ a sloping stroke; if (ων), anomalously far to left

[1] In schol. Ven. Aristoph. *Pax* 140 the same mistake, Κόρινθ- for Τίρυνθ-, appears to have been made in connexion with the same story.

Fr. 8

```
]ειλετο ουχο [
]αφημιοϲε[.]τω.[
]βαϲταϲε[
]ϊναπαντ[
```

Fr. 8 2 .[, the top of an upright

Fr. 9

```
]..ηνχαλινο[
]ντονυβάδην [
]α ουκεπειϲεν[
]υ[
```

Fr. 9 1].., the foot of an upright, followed by the feet of two strokes suggesting χ, though not as wide apart as in the following χ and elsewhere

Fr. 9 2 τὸν Ὑβάδην: Steph. Byz. Ὕβα· οὕτως ὁ δῆμος τῆς Λεοντίδος φυλῆς. τινὲς δὲ τὸν δῆμον λέγουϲιν Ὑβάδαι. τὰ τοπικὰ ἐξ Ὑβαδῶν, εἰς Ὑβαδῶν, ἐν Ὑβαδῶν. Λύϲανδρος Ὑβάδης (witness to will of Theophrastus) Diog. Laert. v. 57.
3 ἀν(τὶ τοῦ).

Fr. 10

```
]...ωϲπορ.[
].ϲαναρδ[
```

Fr. 10 1]..., the lower part of α, the loop made angular by retouching or conversion; the lower parts of two converging strokes, perhaps λ; the tail of a long-tailed letter .[, an upright 2]., the upper end of a stroke rising from left; υ possible

Fr. 11

```
].αλει[
]μοϲ [
]αλαπο [
'.]ρο [
```

Fr. 11 1]., the end of a stroke from left touching the loop of α near the bottom 3]α retouched or corrected

Fr. 12

```
].ανταικ[
]ανάγυρον[
]εχοντ τον[
'].ηϲ αιτια.[
```

Fr. 12 1]., the tail of a long-tailed letter 4 What I have taken for '] might be the upper end of the right-hand arm of υ]., an upright with slight projections to left at top and bottom .[, the lower part of a stroke rising to right

Fr. 12 2 ἀνάγυρον: ἀνάγυρος was the name of a stinking plant and of a destructive 'hero'. One or other is adduced to explain the proverbial ἀνάγυρον κινεῖν (v. Aristoph. *Lysistr.* 68 c. schol.). Aristophanes wrote a play entitled Ἀνάγυρος.
3 τ(ων).

Fr. 13

```
] [
]. [
].ει[
]ιππ.[
.].ιτου[
5        ]φυ[
```

Fr. 13 1 The upper right-hand arc of a circle 3 .[, ο or ω 4]., the upper right-hand arc of a circle, perhaps having the upper end of ' above

Fr. 14   Fr. 15

```
        .        .                    .        .
   ]κλει .[                        ].[
   ]ολωιε[                         ].ω[
   ]ρόπω[                          ].ἠ[.].. .[
   ]ερπ[                           ]...χ[
                               5   ]η[
        .        .                    .        .
```

Fr. 14 1 .[, the upper end of a stroke descending to right

Fr. 15 1 The foot of an upright   2]., perhaps the upper end of the right-hand branch of *v*   3]., perhaps the end of the cross-stroke of c   ].., an upright, followed by the lower part of an upright descending below the line   4]., the upper right-hand arc of a small circle above the line   Before χ what now looks like φρ, but the tail of ρ is anomalous and should perhaps be assigned to l. 5   5 For η perhaps *v*   There may be an upright (see l. 4) above the left-hand side

2814. Hexameter Poem about a War between Greeks and Persians

There is too little about which there is certainty in the following remnant of a composition in hexameters to make it profitable to spend time on its identification. On the assumption that ll. 27 seq. imply war between Greeks and Persians one's first guess would be that it represents the work of Choerilus of Samos, active towards the end of the fifth century B.C., who is credited with Περσικά (in more than one book) by Herodian (π.μ.λ. ii 919 L.; Περϲηίϲ Stobaeus, *Flor.* iii 27, 1) and with ποιήματα specified as Βαρβαρικά, Μηδικά, Περϲικά in a scrap of papyrus, possibly a colophon, published as **1399**. From the entry in Suidas (ἔγραψε δὲ ταῦτα· τὴν Ἀθηναίων νίκην κατὰ Ξέρξου . . .) it would be inferred, on a strict interpretation, that the Marathon campaign was not included. But hardly anything is known of its contents except the list of the contingents of the Persian army (frr. 3, 4 K).

In **2814** the name of Miltiades is recognizable with fair certainty in l. 16. If l. 29 implies, as I think it does, that the speaker of the foregoing lines was cut off prematurely, it would suit the circumstances of Miltiades' death after his failure against Paros. Then l. 31 might refer to his son Kimon, who appears to have been a well-to-do person, such as the promises set out in ll. 33 seqq. may be taken to imply. But who the speaker of the whole is supposed to be I cannot guess.

The hypothesis is obviously very precarious. There were other struggles between Greeks and Persians, and the signs of lateness in the language (ll. 27, 34), if not fatal to the attribution to Choerilus, are not favourable to it.

The hand is a tolerably well-formed example of a common type assigned to the second century, but there is from place to place a noticeable irregularity in the size and thickness of the letters (e.g. ll. 29 seqq.). The text contains a good number of mistakes, some corrected, some (ll. 21, 30, 33) not. There are a few elisions marked and stops in the high and median position, but no accents.

The material condition of the piece is extremely poor. Apart from the fact that the ink is in many places rubbed or faded, the surface is loose and liable to flake off, which it has done in some places where I may not have relocated it exactly and in others where it is lost.

].δεποσισμεθε[
].τ᾽.πιχθονιων[
]επειη[]ουτισε[
].....[..]νερυκεμεν·[
].υσινεριζεμενου[
]οντεσεναcπ[..].ν·η[
]ντεσο.ηςγεγααc[
].ιμενο.ουσυναρηξ[
].cσινεπειβρισηστρα[
].....σουλα[.]cμολ[].[
].....[....]εμεναι[
]..νοισιν [   ]...ιπ[
]..μ.[   ]....[.].εμ[
].χαν[.]..ν[].....[].ε[.]ε.αιλ[
]νκλεοσεc[   ]ενισποιμ[
].αδου[].ο.[   ]αμονενμ.[
].λ.μ.[   ]...[]..c.ιπλ[
]αγα[.].αλ.[.].[   ].σιληοσα..[
]εγερουμο[.].γαρ.[].[.]ουλουδ.π[
].κωντρηχιαν.[   ]..ναναεταουσιν·
].εσοιποντοιπαρε[.]χατιαισιν[.]μονται·
]δεσαγχιβεβ[ ]εσο...[ ]νητορεχοντεc.
].δαυτωνδιχα[ ]μος.ν.[ ].ο[.]..ινο..[
]...[.].ζωεc.[ ]ρ̣.δενυ.[]μ.φ.[].[
..]υμεωνστρα[..]ηνσυνα[.]ειρεμενευτε[
]δευησεινδουκα[.]ποτ᾽[.].περχομενωνεπ[.]κο.[
.]αονδευρωπ[.]cπανεπαρ..ονεμμεν[.].[
.]ερσαις....[.]...ευτος[.]ο.στρ...ναιχ[
]καικενδη..[..].εστοταδη'αγορευ[.].....[
]ειμημινκατ.πεφνεεπερ[.]ομενηδιοσαι[
].υνδεπαιc[..].[.].νενφρενασαλκιμοσουκ.[
]ωδετ.ρηλυθη·[..]υιδουδ᾽ιοτητινεεσθω[
]υμειωνδουδε.ετποσχεσιηνδετελεσσει [
]μουνονεφεσπ[.].ενοιc·αδ᾽επαρκιαδωτινη[
]ε[[ν]]γαρω[[π]]οπας.[].πο[[κ]]᾽...ητρησινεκαστω[
]οινουδουκενε[.]ειτατοσοσστρατοσουδετι[

```
          ]ηδε πόcιc μεθε[
          ]ατ’ ἐπιχθονίων[
          ]επειη[]ωτιcε[
      ]....[..]ν ἐρυκέμεν [
  5   ].υcιν ἐριζέμεν ου[
      ]οντεc ἐν ἀcπ[ίc]ιν, η[
      ]ντεc ὀμῆc γεγάαc[
      ].ιμενο. ου cυναρηξ[
      ]εccιν ἐπεὶ βρίcηι cτρα[
 10   ]....cουλα[.]c μολ[].[
      ]....[....]εμεναι[
      ]..νοιcιν[     ].cιπ[
      ]ορημο[    ]ναρι[.]τεμ[
      ]ιχαν[.].δν[].cε..[.]κε[.].ε.αιλ[
 15   ]ν κλέοc εc[    ]ένιcποιμ[
   Μιλ]τιάδου .ο.[    ].αμον εν μ.[
      ]αλαμι[       ]...[]..c.ι πλ[
      ]αγα[.].αλ.[.].[        β]αcιλῆοc α..[
      ]ετέρου μο[.].ναρ.[    ]α[.]ουλουδ.π[
 20   ].κων τρηχεῖαν .[    ].ονα ναετάουcιν,
      ].εc οἳ Πόντοι⟨ο⟩ παρ’ ἐ[c]χατίαιcι ν[έ]μονται,
   Ἀρκά]δεc ἄγχι βεβ[ῶτ]εc ὀμοι[..ο]ν ἦτορ ἔχοντεc.
      ].δ’ αὐτῶν δίχα[..]μοc..ν.[    ]μο[.].cινου.[
      ]εκο[.].ζωεcβ[        ]ῥ.δενυ.[]μυφ.[]..[
 25   ..]ὑμέων cτρα[τι]ὴν cυνα[γ]ειρέμεν εὖτε[
   δευήcειν δ’ οὐκ ἄ[ν] ποτ’ [ἐ]περχομένων ἐπ[ι]κού[ρων,
   λ]αὸν δ’ Εὐρώπ[η]c πανεπάρκιον ἔμμεν[.]..[
   Π]έρcαιc ..υ.[.]...εν τόc[c]ον cτρατὸν αἰχ[μητάων.
   καί κεν δὴ τε[τέ]λεcτο τάδ’ ἦι ἀγορευc[.]..υ..[  ,
 30   εἰ μή μιν κατέπεφνε⟨ν⟩ ἐπερ[χ]ομένη Διὸc αἶ[cα.
   νῦν δὲ πάιc[..].[.].νεν φρέναc ἄλκιμοc οὐκ.[
   ὧδέ τ’ ἐρητύθη·[..]νιδου δ’ ἰότητι νεέcθω.
   ὑμείων δ’ οὐ δεύεθ’ ὑποcχεcίην δὲ τελέccει
   μοῦνον ἐφεcπο[μ]ένοιc, τὰ δ’ ἐπάρκια δωτίνη[
 35   ἐκ μεγάρων ὀπάcε[ι] ποτ’ ..ῥήτρηιcιν ἑκάcτω[ι,
   οἴνου δ’ οὔ κεν ἔ[π]ειτα τόcοc cτρατὸc οὐδέ τι[
```

There is a 'joint' down the middle of the column

3 Rubbed; the dotted letters might be others of similar outline   There is room for a letter after η in a worm-run but no certainty that one was written   4]....[, the third letter might be circular. It is preceded by the foot of an upright serifed to left. The first is represented by a flat trace on the line, the fourth by a dot below the line   5]., on the underlayer; perhaps an arc of the lower left-hand side of ο   8]., prima facie the right-hand part of the loop of ρ   Between ο and ο possibly μ, but the surface is too much damaged for any letter to be verifiable   9 Of]ϛ only two specks presumably representing the overhang and the turn-up   10].., on a single fibre two dots and a horizontal stroke just off the base-line   Before ϲω what now looks like a crescent facing to left, followed by a stumpy upright   ].[, a dot level with the top of the letters   11]....[, a dot level with the top of the letters, followed at an interval by the top of an upright, then the top of a circle and perhaps the upper parts of the diagonal and the right-hand upright of ν   12]..ϛ, the base of a circle, followed by what might be the underside of the loop of α   13 Of]τ no trace of the left-hand part of the cross-stroke   14].δ, a dot on the line, followed by the base and right-hand angle of δ?].ϛ, on the line the right-hand end of a stroke slightly tilted from left, followed by a flattened ϲ?   ..[, apparently ρρ possible   Of]κ only the right-hand ends of the branches   Between]ϛ (for which θ not ruled out) and α a speck on the line, nearer α   16]τι   see comm.   Before ο a heavy dot below the line, after ο three dots one above another presumably representing an upright   ]., the lower part of an upright with ink on both sides; perhaps more than one letter   .[, perhaps the tip of the loop of α   17 Of]αλα only the base-cusps, except for the tip of the right-hand stroke of λ   Of ι[only the foot]...[, on the line two converging strokes, like the lower part of χ, followed by the lower part of a stroke rising to right, and this by the foot of an upright and a dot to its right on the line   ].., the foot of an upright, followed by the lower left-hand arc of ε or ϲ   Between ϲ and ι very faint the top of a circle   18 Of]α the juncture of the loop and the tail   ]., on the line a stroke slightly tilted from left   After αλ dispersed traces which I may well have wrongly distributed   ..[, an upright, perhaps π, or possibly ν, followed by faint traces near the line   19 The cross-stroke of γ does not come up to the upright, still less cross it to form τ   The loop of ρ has nearly vanished   ]., the right-hand arc of a circle, thickened at the top; ο not suggested   .[, the foot of an upright   Of]ρ only the left-hand part   Between δ and π a speck level with the top of the letters, followed by the top of an upright at a slightly lower level   20]., a thick upright, perhaps not a letter [Now detached and lost]   .[, if ink, a trace level with the top of the letters   ].ρ, the upper part of an upright hooked to right at top, followed by a dot from the middle of the left-hand side and an arc from the lower part of the right-hand side of a circle   21]., the lower part of a stroke descending with a curve from left   22 μ represented only by the upper parts of the central strokes and doubtfully the tail of the right-hand stroke   23]., a trace on a single fibre   ]μρϲ the ρ anomalous;].μνϲ might be a better interpretation   Between ϲ and ν apparently the left-hand half of a small ε or ϲ, followed by a short horizontal stroke on the line; there is not room for two full-sized letters   After ν perhaps elements of an upright, but the fibres are in disorder   Of]μ only the right-hand stroke   ]., the top of a small loop, to right of which a trace against the back of ϲ   Of ν only the fork; perhaps χ possible   .[, most resembles the loop of ρ, but angular; perhaps touches a letter following to right   24 Of ϛκρ only the lower parts   ]., perhaps the top and base and the right-hand end of the cross-stroke of ε   β[, anomalous, the upper loop inordinately small. The straight interpretation of the ink is: a small ο perched on the left-hand element of π   Over]ρ a slightly convex upright   Before δ the fibres disordered; perhaps a single ν, perhaps two letters represented by an upright with a projection to left of its top and specks to right, and the upper end of a stroke descending to right   .[, the lower part of a stroke rising to right Of ν between]μ and φ only the stalk   After φ an upright with ink to right of its top   ]..[, an upright, followed by a short flat stroke level with the top of the letters and a dot diagonally opposite to right on the line   25 The appearance at the end of the line of the left-hand end of a cross-stroke as of τ is illusory   27]..[, specks, followed by the top and bottom of an upright descending below the line; above, a dot and the tip of an upright, apparently interlinear   28 Between ϲ and ν (of which only the fork) the upper end of a stroke descending to right, followed by the top of a circle   .[, a dot level with the top of the letters   ]..., the right-hand end of a cross-stroke, as of γ, followed by the upper end of a stroke descending to right, between them on the line the base of a circle; before ε what could be taken for a damaged μ, but the surface is much disturbed and not all the ink is accounted for   29 .[,

the left-hand arc of a circle   ]..., the base of ε or ϲ, followed by two dots on the line which may represent one letter   Of υ the right-hand arm is lost. There is a dot, which does not seem to be part of a *trema*, above the left-hand arm   ..[, traces level with the top of the letters   31 The first ν of νῦν is unsatisfactory, as a horizontal stroke on the line is not accounted for   ].[, a dot level with the top of the letters   ]., a short thick upright; ο not suggested, but perhaps possible   .[, the base of a circle?   32 τερ, unless it was τορ, seems to have been written originally. A large ε in a different style is written on the original vowel   λ, τ appears to be in the same hand as the rest; λ is not cancelled   .[, a dot about mid letter   Of]ρι only the upper part of the diagonal of ν and the extreme lower end of ι   33 Of υ nothing but the extreme tips of the arms   υ looks inserted *currente calamo*   34 τα I am not sure that τ is not illusory and that ᾶ should not be written   35 ϲ.[, a dot on the line   ]., a trace like the back of the loop of ρ   Above the cancelled κ a small τ, having lost the left-hand part of its bar, and a dot about mid letter   ..., in a thinner pen the top of a stroke rising to right and the upper part of an upright; close to the second an upright of the usual thickness; two dots apparently representing the top and bottom of an upright with blanks on either side   36 τα α rewritten

I cannot contribute much to the understanding of these verses either in the very defective upper part of the column or the almost continuous lower part. The following disjointed observations may be worth making.

8 ϲυναρήγειν not recorded.

9 or ἐπ{ε}ιβρίϲηι?

16 The stalk of τ projects through the cross-stroke, of which the left-hand part is lost, so that the ink now looks more like η than anything else. If Μιλτιάδου is right, ἐν Μα[ραθῶνι may be considered for the end of the verse (though Μαραθῶνι appears to be far more usual than ἐν Μαραθῶνι in references to this action).

17 The letters, if correctly read, suggest Ϲαλαμίϲ in some form.

Ἐ]λλήνεϲϲι πλ[appears compatible with the remains, though I should have expected to see the lower end of the diagonal of ν.

18 seq. The presence of ετερου, if it is rightly recognized, and if it represents ἑτέρου or a compound (not ἡμ-, ὑμ-, which I think are too short), suggests the view that βαϲιλῆοϲ refers to a Spartan, not to the Persian, king.

20 The object of ναετάουϲιν I suppose to be the preceding word. If]μονα could be read—I can neither verify it nor rule it out—Λακεδαίμονα would seem to me a reasonable guess. I can make no suggestion for the residual].κων.

21 seq. The absence of conjunctions seems to indicate that these are successive entries in a list.

21 In isolation I should have taken this verse to be Θρήϊ]κεϲ, οἳ Πόντοιο παρ' ἐϲχατίαιϲι νέμονται. (The ν ἐφελκυϲτικόν at the end of l. 20 is not in favour of Θρη- but not fatal to it.) But how can Arcadians be described as ἄγχι βεβῶτεϲ to Thracians? As far as I see, some difficulties would disappear if ll. 21–2 were transposed. Arcadians would then be next perhaps to Laconians. But too much is uncertain to make guessing attractive.

παρ' ἐϲχατίαιϲι is a form of locution I have not found elsewhere. ἐπ' ἐϲχ- is regular and seems more logical; 'on the fringe of' *or* 'beside'.

-ίαιϲι, but -τρηϲιν l. 35.

22 Though Ἀρκάδεϲ is not the only ethnic of dactylic scansion ending in -δεϲ, I do not suppose that the likelihood of its occurrence in this place will be disputed.

The correspondence of participles in this verse to a relative clause in the preceding supports the interpretation of the names as items of a list.

From ναετάουϲιν and νέμονται I infer that ἄγχι βεβῶτεϲ means 'occupying a neighbouring country' not 'next in the line'. Parallel to this 'like in spirit' would not be amiss, but ὁμοίϊον is not prima facie long enough.

25 seqq. A speech, and, to judge by the fact that the speaker is said to be dead in l. 30 but ll. 33 seqq. are obviously still part of a speech, a reported speech. I cannot tell how far above l. 25 it begins. The speakers of both appear to be on the Greek side, but they refer to Greeks with ὑμ-, ll. 25, 33, not ἡμ-.

26 I take the statement to be 'will never lack acceding allies'. This involves the postulation of ἄν

with the future, but though it might be preferable to *construe* 'will miss allies who are never going to turn up', the context, so far as I understand it, rules this out. The suspect construction, to be sure, is introduced by the supplement, but can any of the theoretical alternatives to α[ν] be entertained?

27 λαὸν Εὐρώπης: cf. Ἑλλάδος ϲτρατόν **2625** fr. 1, 1 *c. not.* But it is not certain that the two words are to be taken together here.

πανεπάρκιος recorded only in a defective quotation in Suidas Παλαμήδης. ἐπάρκιος, l. 34, also rare, and late.

28 δ' οὐ γ[ε]γάμεν? 'that the Persians have not acquired'. This infinitive at Pind. *Ol.* ix 110 and in composition at *Il.* v 248, xx 106.

Cf. *Il.* viii 472 Ἀργείων πουλὺν ϲτρατὸν αἰχμητάων.

30 κατέπεφνεν ἐπερχομένη: cf. ἐποιχόμενος, -μένη, κατέπεφνε regularly in Homer (*Il.* xxiv 759, *Od.* v 124, et al.).

Διὸς αἶϲα Homeric, but not frequent, e.g. *Il.* xvii 321, *Od.* ix 52.

31 πάις 'his son'?

φρένας ἄλκιμος, if that is to be recognized, strikes me as a peculiar locution and I can find no support nearer than τοῦ δ' ἐν φρεϲὶν ἄλκιμον ἦτορ *Il.* xvii 111.

32 ὧδέ τ' ἐρητύθη 'so he was checked'. I do not see to what this can refer where it stands. Next to l. 30 it would present no difficulty.

I do not see any case to be made for ἔτ(ι).

Κρονίδου δ' ἰότητι? I cannot verify it and cannot clearly see the bearing. Although he was stopped for the time being, may he come, God willing, later on?

33 Prima facie 'he has no need of you', but this seems rather inconsequent and I suspect that δεύϲεθ' was intended with the sense 'he will not fall behind you', do less than you; cf. *Il.* xxiii 483 ἀλλά . . . πάντα δεύεαι Ἀργείων, sim. v 636.

33 seq. ὑποϲχεϲίην . . . τελέϲϲει . . . ἐφεϲπομένοις cf. *Od.* x 483 τέλεϲόν μοι ὑπόϲχεϲιν.

μοῦνον: presumably 'if you do but . . .' not 'only if'.

ἐφεϲπομ-: this false form appears in late hexameters. If the present text is rightly attributed to Choerilus it is by a good deal the earliest example.

I suppose ἐπάρκια δωτίνη[ϲιν: cf. οὐϲίαν ταῖς δαπάναις ἐπαρκῆ Plut. *Cic.* 7.

35 I can give no satisfactory account of ποτ' in the context nor guess the two letters before ῥήτρηϲιν. There is no room for ἐπί, as at Callim. fr. 85, 6.

2815. DIONYSIUS, Γιγαντιάς BOOK I (AND OTHERS?)

Nothing is known about the Γιγαντιάς except what can be elicited from the five places where it is referred to in Stephanus Byzantinus. From these it appears that it was a composition in hexameters[1] consisting of not less than three books, in each of which there was some mention of Thessaly (Steph. Byz. in Δώτιον and Νέϲϲων). In Book I there was also a mention of a Locrian town not otherwise recorded, Κελαδώνη. The recurrence of this name in Fr. 9 of the following collection of pieces of hexameter verse is the chief reason, the Thessalian location of the matter in Fr. 2 a secondary argument, for identifying the Γιγαντιάς in their source. But if this is so, they do not afford much positive information about its subject. Nothing that I see has any particular relevance to the story of the Giants, and indeed 'Story of the Giants' should by analogy be Γιγαντίς,[2] not Γιγαντιάς, of which the natural interpretation would be 'Story of Γιγαντία', though perhaps this argument should not be pressed.

[1] Stephanus quotes from it two unconnected hexameters. This leaves open the theoretical possibility that it was in elegiacs, which cannot be disproved but I suppose is not at all likely.

[2] The forms Ἰλιάς, Μιννάς are exceptional and are to be accounted for by the nature of the penultimate vowel.

The name of the author of the Γιγαντιάς is given by Stephanus as Dionysius. If this is the περιηγητής, to whom a piece defined as γιγαντίων is, along with others, ascribed in the *uita Chis.* (Accad. Naz. Linc. *Bollettino* N.s. v p. 10),[1] if the date of the περιηγητής is rightly inferred from his acrostich (περιηγ. 112 seqq., 522 seqq.) to fall in the first half of the second century, and if the fragments here presented are rightly referred to the Γιγαντιάς, this manuscript has the interest of being an approximately contemporary copy of the work that it contains.

The author, whoever he was, had not, so far as I can judge from the incomplete verses that survive, a strongly marked style, and leans more on the old than the Hellenistic epic.

The text is written in a bold upright round hand of a type ascribed to the second century. The want of standardization in the form of many letters and their reduction in size towards the bottom of the column dispose me to think that the writer may not have been a professional copyist.

---

[1] γέγραπται δὲ καὶ αὐτῷ καὶ λιθιακὰ βιβλία διοσημείων τε καὶ γιγαντίων ἕτερα . . .

Fr. 1

(*a*)   ].α.[]αιουϲιπολ ηαϲ[

      ].φροϲυνητεδικητε[

      ]ι·ζευϲδεκρατοϲαιεν.[

      ]ενοϲεπλετοκηραϲαλ[

5   ]εξαλοϲ·ενδεθεμιϲτα[

      ].ιϲϲοοανθρωποιϲι[

      ]διοϲεπιτελ[   ]εν.[

      ]εεινδ.[

      ].ολεμ[

10   ].νκρατ[   ]...[ ]..[

      ]ηυπερυβριο[.]εξει [

      ]ηθαμαθωρηϲ..ντ[

      ]αναλκειηντελελογ[

      ]εχεφροϲυνηιϲινο.[

15   ]ερφιαλοϲμαλεουϲ[

      ].αδιοιοαναϲϲων [

      ].ιϲενινη.[ ].το.[

                 ]ϲ   [

                 ]η.[

(*b*)   ·   ·   ·

      ]...[].[

      ]εοιενπυρ[

      ]φετερηιεν.[

      ]ϲμονορινεται.ηεπιλ[

5   ]ιϲηαϲχετονοινοβ[

      ]ειραϲενανδραϲινο.[.].[

      ]ταμεν[.]ομονεπρη[

      ].αιϲχοϲελ[..].ειητεφ[.]λοιϲ[

Fr. 1 (*a*), (*b*) These two fragments have no horizontal fibres in common. It is not possible to determine how many lines are lost between (*a*) 19 and (*b*) 1

(*a*) 1]., ink resembling the bottom angle of ν but having a diagonal stroke across the opening   .[, the lower part of an upright; a normally broad letter, e.g. ν, would be expected to be partly visible between this and α   2]., a flat trace on the line   3 .[, perhaps the upper left-hand curve of ε or ο   6]., the lower end of a stroke descending from left   7 .[, the top left-hand arc of a circle   8 .[, α seems likeliest   9]., a dot on the line   10]., the right-hand arc of a circle   ]..[, a loop, open to left, on the line, suggesting β, followed by the lower part of an upright, and this at an interval by the lower left-hand arc of a circle   ].[, the bases of two circles on the line; possibly a single ω   12 After c no doubt co but scarcely represented   14 .[, the left-hand arc of a circle   16]., the right-hand end of a stroke touching the top of the loop of α; τ not suggested   17]., the top of a circle   .[, an upright with the start of a stroke to right at its centre; η not κ suggested   ., on the line the foot of a stroke curling to right   .[, the left-hand arc of a circle   19 .[, the top of an upright

(b) 1]...[, a dot on and a dot just below the line, followed by the lower part of an upright   ].[traces on the line, perhaps two letters   3 .[, the lower part of an upright, followed by a dot on the line; π or ι.[suitable   6 .[, the foot of a stroke descending just below the line with a slight slope to left   ].[, the foot of an upright   8]., the end of a stroke touching the bottom of the loop of α]., a dot on the line

Fr. 1 (a) 2 The first letter can hardly be other than ο or ω, so that cα]οφροсύνη (*Od.* xxiii 13, 30) or c]ωφροсύνη (Theogn. 379, al.) looks likely.

3 ὀ[φελλ-? còν δὲ κράτος αἰὲν ἀέξειν *Il.* xii 214. Or ὀ[πάζειν in some form?

4 κῆρας followed by some form of ἀλύσκειν frequent in *Odyssey* and a few examples in *Iliad.*

5 Presumably ἐξ ἁλός. But at *Od.* xi 134, xxiii 281 there was an ancient view that ἔξαλος should be read, ὡς ἔκβιος, οἷον ἠπειρωτικòς καὶ οὐ θαλάσσιος.

6 πο]λισσόον only *hy. Hom.* viii. 2, of Ares. But θέμιστα[ς, l. 5, suggests that the qualification perhaps applies to some abstract, such as e.g. justice. εἰρήνην... cαόπτολιν Nonn. *Dion.* xli 395.

7 Διὸς ἐπιτελ[λομ]ένο[ιο acceptable.

11 On the basis of Hes. *Op.* 217 δίκη δ' ὑπὲρ ὕβριος ἴσχει a reasonable guess is δίκ]η ὑπὲρ ὕβριο[ς] ἔξει.

12 θωρήσσοντ[-.

13 ἀναλκείην τε λελογ[χ-: the locution is parallel to those found with parts of κτάομαι (the commonest: Soph. *Antig.* 924 τὴν δυσσέβειαν ... ἐκτησάμην, Eur. *I.T.* δειλίαν ... καὶ κάκην κεκτήσομαι, *Med.* 218 ἐκτήσαντο ... ῥᾳθυμίαν), φέρω (Soph. *Electr.* 968 seq. εὐσέβειαν ... οἴσει), λαμβάνω (Eur. *Ion* 600 μωρίαν ... λήψομαι), but I can adduce no similar example of the employment of λαγχάνω.

ἀναλκείησι three times in the *Iliad,* but the singular recorded only once, Theogn. 891.

14 ἐχεφροσύνησι see on fr. 4, 2.

15 ὑπ]ερφίαλος μάλ' ἐοῦς[α, but this strikes me as odd enough to justify the search for a genitive in μαλεους[, parallel to].αδίοιο in l. 16 and like it governed by ἀνάσσων. But I can find nothing.

17]οις ἔνι νηή[σα]ντος acceptable.

(b) 3 c]φετέρηι ἔνι .[one possibility.

4 οὐ κατὰ κό]σμον ὀρίνεται to some extent suggested by the next line.

4 seq. ἢ ἐπιλ[   ]ις ἢ ἄσχετον οἰνοβ[αρείων.

ἄσχετον adverbial Ap. Rhod. *Argon.* iv 1738. οἰνοβαρείων only *Od.* (3 times), but οἰνοβαρέω also Theogn. 503.

8 αἰσχος ἐλ[εγ]χείη τε φ[ί]λοις[ι: cf. *Od.* xviii 225 σοί κ' αἰσχος λώβη τε ... πέλοιτο. But perhaps I should remark that it is possible that αἰσχος attaches to a different person from ἐλεγχείη.

ἐλεγχείη: *Il.* xxiii 408 μὴ σφῶιν ἐλεγχείην καταχεύηι, *Od.* xiv 38, al.

Fr. 2

(*a*)

      .   .   .

].ιο.[

]ντοςυν[.].·[.]νιδη..[

]ομαχοιλα.[..]αιμεπ[

]αςςονταμἑηςυπε[

   5   ]α.φαλεη.ηςφινπ[

]πολεμοιοδορυς[

].παδεν....ικεκλη.[   ]ν[

]ωνεπι[.....]ο.[.]χηρεμακυςςε[.]εμ..ο[

]αδαιγιμιοντεκαινιεαςαιγιμοι[]   [

 10 (*b*)   ]τερουςονομηνεδυμανατεπ[.]μφυλον[

       ].δα[   ].αντεςς[.]δικηιεπεοικ[...]μν[.]ον[

       ]μι'...[   ]ικηςευεργες[   ] [

       ]ηςτον[   ]εινταδερεξετα[(*c*)]..[   ].[

      ]οταςτ.[   ]ειοδιαπραθεειν.[   ]ωτ.   [

 15   ].πετ.[   ]ωντιταρω[..].[   ]ωνου   [

      ].ει[   ]τ[ ]λιεθραν[   ]θα.[

      ]ω.[   ]πατρωϊον[ ]..[

].···[].ολυνθαμ[.].αονοπαςςαμ[

]καιηνπ[..]αθεςφατ'ιωςιν[

 20   ]τεκαιε.[..]αγυιανϊθωμ[

]ςικελευθοις.   [

].μεναιτεκεεςς[

].οιρηςωντα[

Fr. 2 The level of (*b*) relatively to (*a*) is fixed by cross-fibres. I cannot follow fibres of the back of (*a*) into (*b*) and so cannot fix the interval between them. The level of (*c*) relatively to (*a*) is likewise fixed by cross-fibres and again I cannot certainly follow fibres of the back from (*a*) into (*c*), but the interval between them may be fairly closely determinable by internal evidence; see note on l. 14

1]., traces suggesting the upper right-hand arc of a circle   .[, a dot on the line   2]..[, on the line the base of a small circle, followed by a dot at a slightly lower level   ..[, I think ι followed by the lower left-hand arc of a circle, but a rather large π may be possible   3 .[, apparently ι with a dot below   5 Between α and φ what now resembles γ slightly tilted backwards   ϛ damaged, θ perhaps not ruled out   Between η and η a trace on the line   7]., a dot level with the top of the letters, some way from π   After ν a headless upright, before ι a sinuous upright suggesting η; between them two dots level with the top of the letters   .[, a thick dot a little below mid-letter   Of]ν[only the feet   8 Of]ω only the base of the first circle and the lower right-hand arc of the second;].ο could be read   .[, a trace on the line   After μ the foot of an upright, prima facie ι, followed at an interval by the lower part of a circle, prima facie θ   10 Of π[only the top left-hand angle

11 (b)]., a dot just below the line   (a)]., a cross-stroke level with the top of the letters   12 (b) . . . [, the left-hand arc of a circle, followed by the foot of an upright and the bottom left-hand arc of a circle, perhaps a single π   13 (c)]..[, the foot of an upright crossed by the lower end of a stroke descending from left, followed at an interval by the foot of an upright   ].[, the foot of an upright   14 (b) .[, the upper left-hand arc of a circle a little higher than the top of the letters   (a) .[, a dot level with the top of the letters   (c) After τ a dot on the line   15 (b)]., the lower part of a stroke descending from left and curving up   .[, the left-hand end of a cross-stroke, continuing that of τ, with a trace below as of a stroke descending from it   (a)].[, the upper end of a stroke descending steeply to right   16 (a)]., a thin trace above and to left of the upper part of ε   Of]τ[the upper central part; the upper right-hand part of π perhaps not ruled out   (c) .[, the top of an upright   17 (a) .[, the left-hand arc of a circle   (c)]..[, κο seems likeliest, but I should have expected, in spite of damage, to see some of the upper branch of κ; for o not, I think, c   18 (a)]...[, the first letter perhaps c, but represented only by the right-hand end of the overhang, the third ε or θ; between these a dot level with the top of the letters   (c)]., a trace below the line, not particularly suggesting π   ]., the lower end of a stroke descending from left   20 .[, a dot level with the top of the letters   22]., the top of a circle   23]., the right-hand arc of a small circle against the left-hand side of o, which is abnormally small

Fr. 2 I can make very little of this as a whole or in detail. I offer a few remarks on points that have occurred to me as representing possible lines of inquiry.

2 μα]ντοϲύν[η]..[, or -]ντο (e.g. γέ-, θέ- ντο) cὺν [.]..[.]ν-?
Κρ[ο]νίδηι, -δηιϲ[ι could be accepted.

3 As λα.[..]αι looks as if it might be the plural of a first declension name, it may be remarked that Λαπ[ίθ]αι is not a possible *reading*, though a mention of them would be congruous with the mention of Aegimius below. See also on l. 15. I do not know what is meant by the dot under ι[. A cancellation is ordinarily denoted by a dot over the cancelled letter.

No Greek word is known to begin with μεπ-. μετ.[is not to be read. It seems that one must operate with με, in which case this will be part of a speech.

5 I find it hard to believe that]αρφ- was written, but nothing else as likely as καρφαλέη. seems to offer. At *Il.* xxi 541 δίψηι καρχαλέοι with variants καρφαλέοι, καρχαλέη suggests a possible supplement.

6 If πολέμοιο δορυϲ[ϲόου, Theogn. 987 δορυϲϲόον ἐϲ πόνον ἀνδρῶν is to be compared. But a context can be thought of in which e.g. δορυϲϲόοι would be apposite, and then the parallel would be with [Hes.] *Scut.* 54 δορυϲϲόωι Ἀμφιτρύωνι.

8 The likely, though not the only theoretically available, articulation is]χ' ἠρέμα κύϲϲε[, the last two words not necessarily construed together. What follows it should be possible to make out, but I can neither account for the space between the two dotted letters nor suggest a suitable object for κύϲϲε.

9 seq. The Thessalian King Aegimius appears in Greek legend as a beneficiary and benefactor of Herakles and father of Dyman and Pamphylus, eponyms of two of the three Dorian tribes. ἀμφο]τέρουϲ therefore may be taken as likely and defines the left-hand alignment of the column.

Αἰγίμιόν τε . . . ὀνόμηνε Δυμᾶνά τε Π[ά]μφυλόν [τε. Since it is clear that ὀνόμηνε cannot here mean 'gave their names to', I suppose it means 'nominated' or the like. I see no clue to the subject, but I suppose he might be Herakles.

11 -άντεϲϲι δίκηι ἐπεοικ[ότα] μῦ[θ]ον 'an utterance such as justice required'. I have found no other instance of ἐπεοικώϲ, ἐπεικώϲ in any form but the neuter plural.

14 διαπραθέειν μ[εμα]ῶτα indicated by comparison with *Il.* xi 733 ἄϲτυ διαπραθέειν μεμαῶτεϲ, *Il.* ix 532, Hes. *Scut.* 240, *Catal.* fr. 35, 3. The interval assumed suits the assumption of π]τ[ο]λίεθρα in l. 16 and requires a supplement of 5 or 6 letters before]ωνου in l. 15.

Since ἄϲτυ might be looked for hereabouts, it must be said that it cannot be read in (b). ἀϲτε[may be possible, though I do not think it would be the first choice.

15 Τίταρω[ν(-): Steph. Byz. Τιταρών· πόλιϲ Θεϲϲαλίαϲ ἦν Τίταρον Λυκόφρων φηϲί (*Alex.* 904). τὸ ἐθνικὸν Τιταρώνιοϲ. A third form of the name is recognized in Strabo's τὸ Τιτάριον ὄροϲ, which he says is a continuation of Mount Olympus (vii 329 frr. 14, 15; ix 441). In view of the information supplied by Diodorus (iv 37): πολέμου ϲυνεϲτῶτοϲ Δωριεῦϲι τοῖϲ τὴν Ἑϲτιαιῶτιν καλουμένην οἰκοῦϲιν, ὧν ἐβαϲίλευεν

Αἰγίμιος, καὶ τοῖς Λαπίθαις τοῖς περὶ τὸν Ὄλυμπον ἱδρυμένοις, ὧν ἐδυνάστευε Κόρωνος κτλ., it is reasonably likely that Κορ]ώνου should be recognized here.[1]

In view of the dialectal Πετθ- for Θεσσ- I may as well remark that it is not recognizable here.

16 π]τ[ο]λίεθρα see on l. 14. ν[έεσ]θαι?

17 πατρώϊον [οἶ]κο[ν will be thought of, but οι looks hardly broad enough for the space.

18 πολύν θ' ἅμα λαὸν ὀπάσσαι after *Il.* xviii 452 πολὺν δ' ἅμα λαὸν ὄπασσε, cf. xvi 38.

19 καὶ ἦν π[αρ]ά . . .? 'If they transgress . . .'.

20 εὐ[ρυ]άγυιαν Ἰθώμην Steph. Byz. Ἰθώμη· πόλις Θεσσαλίας τῆς Πελασγιωτίδος. At *Il.* ii 729 seq. mentioned along with Τρίκκην and Οἰχαλίην, one or both of which may have preceded here.

22 ε- or ο- μεναι τεκέεσσ[ι, probably an infinitive as e.g. *Il.* xii 222 δομέναι τεκέεσσιν ἑοῖσιν.

23 (δια)]μοιρήσωντα[ι hardly avoidable but μ by no means what would have been chosen. The compound at *Od.* xiv 434, Ap. Rhod. *Argon.* i 395.

---

[1] It should perhaps be noticed that in Steph. Byz. the next entry after Τιτάρων is: Τιτωνεύς, ὄρος. Διονύσιος Γιγαντιάδος πρώτωι. ὁ οἰκήτωρ Τιτωνεύς. The same mountain is thought to be referred to by Lycophron in the words ἥ τ' ἐπάκτιος στόρθυγξ Τίτωνος (*Alex.* 1404 seq.). If Τιτωνεύς as the name of the mountain had intruded instead of Τίτωνος into Stephanus as a result of confusion with the *ethnicon*, the supplement Τιτ]ώνου might be considered here. But to go by Lycophron it was not in Thessaly.

Fr. 3

(a)
].[
].α.[

(b)
]..νουϲου[
]ι ειδομεν[
]νταιτρα.[

(c)
]θεοϲρ.[
]υϲηάϲτ[
].νδιερη[
].ϲεπ[
5]ϲιναρη[
]αταδεκ[
].νϊϲα[
]κατα[

(d)
].ϲε[
].ατε[
]δαλαπο.[
].ηυτεβου[
5]θρω.[

(e)
].ωι[
.]...δεφλε[
..]κομεναμα[
..]νδηνμενκ[
5 .]μφωδαιτε[
.]...εδηπαν[
]ην[..].εμ.[
]ε.ν[.].καιτρ[
]θαρϲαλεοιϲτε[
10]..ωνπολ[
].ρ.ιυπηελ[
]τωνδετανυ[
]ιχθυεϲαργετα[
]αυτοϲδετρομεωνα.[
15]νηϲαιηιϲϊπποιϲινε[
]οφρα..ϲϲπ.[]ρηνμη[
].ουρηιγλ[
]ωνι·τιϲι.[
]οιοδιαπ[
20]αινοιδο[
[].[ ]

(f)
]παν.[
]ενο.[

(g)
].αορα[
]νεερμεν[
]ουϲαλοϲ[
]κυλ[.]νδετα[
5].αχρηϲουϲ[

(h)
].ϲι[
]ων[

(j)
].αι[
][
][
]τε· υπε[

Fr. 3 (*a*)–(*d*) The relative levels of these four scraps are established by cross-fibres. (*a*) and (*d*) appear to stand on the left of (*b*) and (*c*), but I cannot establish any relation between them or between either and (*b*), (*c*). The interval between (*b*), (*c*) is not determinable by external evidence, but I believe may be fixed within close limits by internal evidence; see on ll. 2 seq.

But a further problem, which I cannot solve, is presented by (*e*). The cross-fibres about ll. 1–4 of this fragment are certainly recognizable about (*d*) 2–5 and (*c*) 5–8. The fibres of the back of the composite (*b*)+(*c*), though I cannot follow any particularly into (*e*), have a strong general resemblance to those of (*e*), left to left and right to right. But if (*b*)+(*c*) is placed so as to give effect to this correspondence, there is too little room for (*d*) between (*e*) and (*c*). If there is no error in these observations, I can only suppose that (*d*) belongs to a different (presumably the preceding) column

(*a*) 1 Two traces on the line suggesting the start of a stroke rising to right and the end of a stroke descending from left, but possibly separate letters   2]., the upper part of the central stroke and a trace of the right-hand side of φ or ψ   .[, two apices; I think μ, but am not sure that λμ could be ruled out

(*b*) 1].., the bottom right-hand arc of a circle followed by the bases of two circles; perhaps three letters represented   Of ν[only the upper end of the left-hand arm   3 .[, the left-hand arc of a circle

(*c*) 1 .[, the lower left-hand arc of a circle   3]., on the line a hook to right   4]., on the line a turn-up, as of ε   7]., the upper part of an upright

(*d*) 1]., the edge of an upright   2]., the lower part of an upright descending below the line 3 .[, the left-hand arc of a circle   4]., the top of an upright   5 .[, the top of a stroke turning over to right but having a hook to left at the turn; not the normal π, perhaps ν

(*e*) 1]., the right-hand end of a horizontal stroke on the line   2]...., the foot of a stroke swinging slightly to right and having a trace to left of its upper end, followed by the bottom left-hand arc of a circle, a dot on the line, the upper and lower ends of the right-hand side of κ or c   6]..., the right-hand end of a cross-stroke level with the top of the letters, the left-hand arc of a circle, a dot level with the top of the letters   7]., a dot on the line   .[, the top of an upright   8 Between ε and ν faint traces, of, I suppose, the top and bottom of ι   ]., a trace above the general level   10].., two traces close together level with the top of the letters   11]., the upper end of a stroke rising with a curve from left   After ρ a similar but heavier stroke with a knobbed upper end   14 .[, the foot of a stroke swinging slightly to right   16 After α apparently the upper tip of a stroke rising from left, followed by what seems to be the top of a circle, though it is rather angular on the left-hand side   After π a thick dot level with the top of the letters. Between this and ν there is a smudge, as of washed-out ink, above the line   17]., the upper tip of a stroke curling up from left   18 .[, the left-hand arc of a circle

(*f*) Apparently from below (*c*), but I can recognize none of the cross-fibres in (*e*) between ll. 6 and 13 1 .[, the left-hand arc of a circle; φ suggested   2 .[, the apex of δ or λ, or perhaps the left-hand apex of μ

(*g*) The fibres of the back seem consistent with a position below the right-hand side of the projecting piece of (*e*)

1]., the lower end of a stroke descending from left   2 Of ν[only the first upright   5]., the right-hand end of a cross-stroke level with the top of the letters

[Addendum. The relation of the following couple of scraps to one another and to frr. (*c*), (*e*), discovered rather late, is, I think, as follows: (*h*) stands directly above (*j*) and represents the ends of (*e*) 1 seq., (*c*) 5 seq. (*j*) follows at an interval of one line and represents the ends of (*e*) 4, (*c*) 8 and of (*e*) 7

(*h*) 1]., a dot on the line

(*j*) 1]., the end of a thin horizontal stroke at mid letter, touching the top of the loop of α   4 *marg.* ε[perhaps a badly made o]

Fr. 3 (*b*)+(*c*) 2 seq. If τραφ[ερ]ην διερη[ν τε is rightly guessed in l. 3, εἰδομέν[ο]υς satisfies the conditions in l. 2.

2 'Like ... or ...' No doubt 'stars', ἄστ[ραςι, the accentuation prescribed by 'the majority and Philoxenus' against ἀςτράςι prescribed by Aristarchus; v. *Il.* xxii 28 c. schol., and 317 codd.

3 τραφ[ερ]ὴν διερή[ν τε: I have found no other example of this pair, the usual pair being τραφερή and ὑγρή (or in the reverse order), *Il.* xxiv 308, *Od.* xx 98, *h. Hom.* ii (Dem.) 43, Oppian. *Cyneg.* i 11

Ap. Rhod. *Argon.* ii 545, iv 281. But Hes. *Op.* 460 exhibits the variant αὕην καὶ διερήν (in a different application).

(*e*) 2 The remains appear consistent with αυθις, but I do not think that this would be aligned with α]μφω in l. 5.

3 ἅμα- is difficult. Hexameter writers lengthen the first syllable of ἀμᾶν (ᾱμᾱειν Hes. *Op.* 392) and lengthen a final short before initial μ (though not, I think, very often before μάλα). ἁμός (or ἀμός) is found in Homer (and elsewhere) for ἐμός. I see no other plausible way of trying to account for the text.

6 ἐ]ξότε acceptable.

12 seq. τῶν δὲ τανυ⟨ ⟩ . . . ἰχθύες ἀργέτα [δημόν: cf. *Il.* xxi 127 ἰχθύς, ὅς κε φάγῃσι Λυκάονος ἀργέτα δημόν. Supply φάγον (*Od.* xiv 135), ἔδονται (*Il.* iv 237), or something of the sort.

The manuscript's accentuation ἀργέτα, I suppose meaning what we write ἀργετά, seems to be idiosyncratic.

15 Νησαίηις ἵπποισι a famous breed of horses to which there are references throughout Greek literature. They appear to be spelt Νισ- as often as Νησ-, and to be stallions at least as often as mares. On their provenience see Stein's note on Hdt. vii 40.

17 (Διὸς)]κούρηι γλ[αυκώπιδι? cf. *Od.* ii 433.

Fr. 4

```
                  •        •
      ]ητέαμνθον[       ]  [
      ]φροσυνηνο[       ] . α . [
      ]νοιειενεφετ[     ]
      ] . αργηστα . [   ]
5     ]υπαλαμηισι[      ]ς
      ]κεφα[ . ]ησδεκαιωμων
      ]αλοιοτενοντα
      ]ροαλησεπιουδει
      ]ντος[ . ]δηρωι
10    ] . ιοντ[ . ]κυπε[ . ]λον
      ]χεναθυπερθε[
```

Fr. 4 2]., an upright with foot hooked up to right and having on left a dot, the end of a stroke, about opposite its centre; perhaps two letters .[, the lower left-hand arc of a circle 4]., the top of a circle .[, the top left-hand arc of a circle 7 Of ạ only the lower side of the loop and the lower part of the right-hand stroke 10]., the lower part of a stroke curving down from left; ε or ϲ likely Of π only the feet, of ϛ only the lower central part of the left-hand side

Fr. 4 1 ἐπ]ητέα μῦθον seems a reasonable guess. ἐπητής, oxytone of the first declension, is found twice in the *Odyssey* (ἐπητής ἐϲϲι καὶ ἀγχίνοος καὶ ἐχέφρων xiii 332, ἐπητῆι ἀνδρὶ ἔοικαϲ xviii 128), oxytone of the third,[1] once in Apollonius Rhodius (*Argon.* ii 987 οὐ γὰρ Ἀμαζονίδες μάλ' ἐπητέες). These are all the literary instances, unless one adds ἐπητέος from *Od.* xxi 306, where it appears from Apoll. *lex. Hom.* in ἐπήτηι (sic) to have been Aristarchus' reading in preference to ἐπητύος.[2] In all these places, however,

---

[1] According to Eustathius (*Od.* xiii 332) the older accentuation was oxytone, the later paroxytone. From schol. *Od.* it appears that Aristarchus, and similarly Herodian, prescribed the oxytone.

[2] Hesych. ἐπητέος· εὐλογιστοῦ, εὐγνώμονος, ϲυνετοῦ, πρᾴου may be based on this.

it is applied to a person. A large assortment of interpretations (partly based on etymological absurdities) is to be found in the scholia and lexica, roughly divisible into those meaning 'with a good head' and those meaning 'with a good heart'.

2]φροςύνη: since *Od.* xiii 332 (above) joins ἐπητής and ἐχέφρων, ἐχε]φροςύνη might be thought of. It was first attested in Agathias (A.P. ix 767) but is now found in fr. 1, 14: since Hesych. in ἐπητής has ςώφρων, λόγιος, κτλ., perhaps ςαο- or ςω]φροςύνη is equally likely. But there are various other possibilities.

3 -μέ]νοι (?) εἶεν ἐφετ[μ-, e.g. μεμνημένοι . . . ἐφετμῆς, cf. Hes. *Op.* 298.

4 Presumably ἀργηςτᾶο.

6 κεφαλῆς δὲ καὶ ὤμων on the model of *Od.* κεφαλῆι τε καὶ ὤμοις (vi 235, and three times in all), κεφαλήν τε καὶ ὤμους (xvii 35, and three times in all); not in *Il.*, though this has similar phrases (ὤμων καὶ κεφαλῆς xi 812, κεφαλήν τε καὶ εὐρέας ὤμους iii 227, ἀπὸ κρατός τε καὶ ὤμων v 7, xvii 205. Presumably '⟨between⟩ head and shoulders'.

7 ἀςτραγ]άλοιο τένοντα. τένοντε or τένοντας would have been usual. What I take to be being described is to be gathered from such passages as *Il.* xiv 465 seq. κεφαλῆς τε καὶ αὐχένος ἐν ςυνεοχμῶι νείατον ἀςτράγαλον, ἀπὸ δ' ἄμφω κέρςε τένοντε, x 455 seq., Hes. *Scut.* 417 seqq., Ap. Rhod. *Argon.* 429 seq.

8 π]ροαλής ἐπὶ οὔδει: I suppose '⟨fell⟩ headlong on the ground', equivalent to πρηνής ἐπὶ γαίηι *Il.* xvi 310, 413, xxi 118. But at *Il.* xxi 262 προαλής is used of sloping ground and at Ap. Rhod. *Argon.* iii 73 of the water coming down a mountain stream.

9]ντο ς[ι]δήρωι.

10 κύπε[λ]λον.

Fr. 5   Fr. 6

```
        •     •   •                              •     •    •
          ] [                                      ]υν.[
      ]μηδειςα[                              ]   ηδαν[
   ]   αλλη[                                 ]   ανερ[
   ]   αζομ[                                 ]   ὸιηδ[
5  ]   ζηνα[                            5    ]   νεὶ.[
   ]α̣λλα.[                                  ]   ανδρ[
   ]  ευταν[                            ]       ωςογ.[
   ]θηλυ[                                    ]   ωρετ.[
     ]ηδ[                                      .]η.υ[
        •     •   •                              •     •    •
```

Fr. 5 6 .[, a dot level with the top of the letters

Fr. 6 1 .[, the lower left-hand arc of a circle below the general level, with two traces to right of its upper end   5 .[, the left-hand arc of a circle, followed by a dot on the line; perhaps more probably two letters   7 .[, the upper left-hand arc of a circle   8 .[, a stroke descending from the end of the cross-stroke of τ   9 After η the upper part of a stroke descending to right

Fr. 7

```
    ].π.[
   ]ιηϲϊ[
  ]ϲφιν[
   ]αυτ[
5  ].ιβο.[
   ].ε.[
```

Fr. 8

```
   ]α[
]  ϲφ[
]  ιερα[
]  ωρ[
```

Fr. 7 1]., a trace on the line   τ headless .[, a dot on the line   5]., a trace at mid letter   .[, the upper left-hand arc of a circle 6]., a trace below the level of the tops of the letters   .[, an upright with serifed foot

Fr. 9

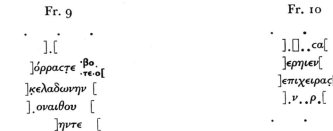

```
    ].[
]όρραϲτε  ·βο·
          .τε·ο[
]κελαδωνην  [
].οναιθου   [
5     ]ηντε    [
```

Fr. 10

```
].[].. .ϲα[
]ερηιεν[
]επιχειραϲ[
].ν..ρ.[
```

Fr. 10 1].[, the foot of a stroke curling to right   ].., the foot of an upright, followed by the lower part of a stroke swinging slightly to right 4]., the top of an upright   After ν either the upper part of ε, or ο; followed by the upper end of a stroke descending to right   .[, the upper part of an upright close to ρ, followed by a dot level with the top of the letters; η[rather than ι.[

Fr. 9 2 marg. 1 .[, prima facie a suspended η 3 Of]κ, only the extreme right-hand ends of the arms   4]., the upper right-hand arc of a circle at mid letter; φ possible but not particularly suggested

Fr. 9 2 The two τε appear to correspond, but the word beginning, if rightly read, with βοη-cannot have corresponded with the word ending with -όρραϲ.
3 Steph. Byz. Κελαδώνη, πόλιϲ Λοκρίδοϲ, ὡϲ Διονύϲιοϲ Γιγαντιάδοϲ πρώτωι.
4 Words ending in -αιθοϲ may be proper names of persons or rivers. I have found none in -(φ)όναιθοϲ.

Fr. 11

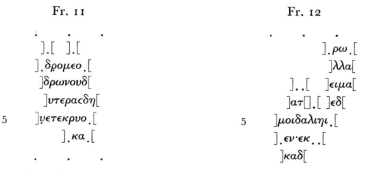

```
     .        .      .
    ].[  ].[
    ].δρομεο.[
   ]δρωνουδ[
   ]υτερασδη[
5  ]υετεκρυο.[
    ].κα.[
        .      .      .
```

Fr. 12

```
         .        .
        ].ρω.[
       ]λλα[
     ]..[   ]ειμα[
    ]ατ[].[  ]εδ[
5   ]μοιδαλιηι.[
    ].εν·εκ..[
   ]καδ[
         .        .
```

Fr. 11 2]., the lower part of an upright hooked to right   .[, the lower part of an upright hooked to left   5 .[, the top left-hand arc of a circle   6 .[, the left-hand arc of ϲ, or possibly o

Fr. 12 1]., the right-hand end of the cross-stroke and a trace of the stalk of γ or τ   .[, the foot of an upright and a trace to its right on the line; perhaps two letters   3]..[, the lower part of an upright descending below the line, with a trace to right of its top, followed by a trace on the line   4].[, the lower part of an upright, perhaps part of a letter to right or left   5 .[, the upper left-hand half of a circle   6]., the right-hand stroke of λ or μ   After κ a triangular letter but anomalous for α, δ, λ   .[, the top left-hand curve of ε or o

Fr. 13

```
     .       .      .
    ].ọ[
   ]νεπ[
    ].νοϲ[
   ]ογαρ[
5   ]..μ[
     .       .      .
```

Fr. 14

```
     .       .      .
    ]. δε̣[
   ]ατοιϲιν[
   ]δενκα.[
    ].με[
5  ]δετυπ[
   ]ϲκọ[
      .       .      .
```

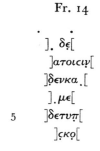

Fr. 13 1]., a trace compatible with the foot of the second upright of ν   For ọ[possibly θ   3]., the right-hand arc of a circle   5].., the top of a circle with a trace close to its right-hand end

Fr. 14 1]., a dot on the line   Of ε̣[only the lower part of the back   4]., what looks like a small ϲ; I think χ likelier

Fr. 15

```
· · ·
].οι.[
].παιδ[
]cτερ.[
].λαμυ[
5    [ ̇ ]
· · ·
```

Fr. 16

```
· · ·
]μεν[
].λοε[
· · ·
```

Fr. 16 2]., the lower end of a stroke descending from left   Of ε[only the upper left-hand part, but not, I think, θ

Fr. 15 1]., faint remains of the feet of two uprights; π possible   .[, a dot on the line   2]., the right-hand ends of the overhang and turn-up of c, or possibly of the branches of κ   3 .[, the lower left-hand arc of a circle   4]., perhaps the right-hand edge of the loop of ρ   Of υ[only the left-hand arm

Fr. 17

```
· · ·
]. .[
]μεν[
· · ·
```

Fr. 18

```
· · ·
]α.[
]υρην[
· · ·
```

Fr. 17 1]., the foot of a stroke curving up to right   .[the turn-up of ε or c

Fr. 18 1 Of]α only the base   .[, two dots on the line

Fr. 19

```
]ενη[
]cαμε[
]ιο  [
]    [
5  ]cετ[
]ηc.[
· · ·
```

Fr. 20

```
]πιμ[
].ιν.[
]αυακ[
]ρπαξ[
5  ]ον[
]τ[
· · ·
```

Fr. 19 Blank above l. 1   6 .[, a loop, en to right, level with the top of the letters

Fr. 20 Blank above l. 1   2]., damaged; perhaps ε likeliest   .[, a short arc of the lower left-hand side of a circle   3 Of]α only the tail; μ not ruled out

Fr. 21

]οδ[
].πα[
]η.[

Fr. 21 2]., the top and bottom of a stroke descending from left

Fr. 22

]α[
]ακελλ[
]ουγα[

Fr. 22 2 For λλ[I am not sure that μ could be ruled out

Fr. 23

].ληιτ[
]..ρυс.[
].οcαυπν[
]νταδεδό[
5   ]..[

Fr. 23 Top of column
1]., the lower part of a stroke descending from left   2].., the lower part of a stroke curving down from left, followed by an upright with traces on both sides of its top; I think υ, but τ not ruled out   .[, ε or θ   3]., an upright with foot turning to right   5 The top of a circle, followed by the upper ends of two strokes descending to right

Fr. 24

].ο.[
]πυρη[

Fr. 24 Blank below l. 2
1]., γ or τ   .[, the left-hand arc of a circle

Fr. 25

]τομ[
]δυω[
].[

Fr. 25 3 The top of a loop

Fr. 26

]μιν[
].ιμα[
]ρην[

Fr. 26 1 Of ν[only the first upright with the upper end of the diagonal   2]., elements near the line of a stroke rising to right

Fr. 27

```
]χερ.[
].-
```

Fr. 27 Blank below l. 2
1 .[, o or c   2]., perhaps the right-hand
ends of the overhang and turn-up of c

Fr. 28

```
]ν..[
]οτερω[
```

Fr. 28 1 Of]ν only the bottom angle   ..[,
the lower part of an upright, followed by a trace
on the line; a single π possible

Fr. 29

```
].
] .[]να[
]οc [
]ρον[
5    ].ικε[
].[] [
```

Fr. 29 1 *marg.* Two traces, perhaps from the
bases of two letters   2 *marg.* .[, perhaps the
loop of α   5]., the right-hand stroke of α or
λ; not, I think, to be combined with ι in ν   6].[,
the top of an upright

Fr. 30

```
]ερρω[.]αν [
].οι        [
```

Fr. 30 2]., perhaps the right-hand edge of
the loop of ρ

Fr. 31

```
]..οχος.[
]ψαμεν.[
]λια[
]μ.[
5    ]η.[
].ε.[
].[
```

Fr. 31 1]., just off the line two strokes
rising slightly to right, the foot of an upright turning out to left close to the second, followed by the
lower part of an upright   For ς possibly ε   .[,
the lower left-hand arc of a circle   2 .[, the
top of an upright   3 Of α[only the lower end
of the loop   4 .[, the left-hand arc of a circle
5 .[, the left-hand arc of a circle   6]. the
lower end of a stroke curving down from left   .[,
γ or π   7 The top of an upright

Fr. 32

```
]ον[
]ουρ[
]να[
].ε.[
5    ]οc[
]μα[
]χρο[
```

Fr. 32 4]., the upper part of a slightly convex upright   .[, a headless upright   7 ο[
damaged; possibly ω

Fr. 33

]ηϊ θε[
]τελλ[
].[

Fr. 33 3 A cross-stroke as of τ

Fr. 34

].υψα.[
]θωο.[

Fr. 34 1]., perhaps the lower part of the loop of ρ   .[, a headless upright   2 .[, λ or the beginning of μ

Fr. 35

]χεμ[
]αγα[
]cθ[

Fr. 35 From below fr. 2 (*a*) or (*b*)?

Fr. 36

]εὐ[
]...[
].cδε[
].ετρα.[
5   ]εcτι.[
].τ.[

Fr. 36 2].., a trace off the line, followed by τ or perhaps γ   .[, the left-hand arc of a circle 3]., the right-hand arc of a circle   4]., a dot level with the top of the letters   .[, an upright 5 .[, a dot on the line   6]., the top of a circle .[, the top of a stroke hooked to left

Fr. 37

]......[
]αζανθει[
]τω.[

Fr. 37 1 The count is uncertain. The bases or lower parts of: a stroke hooked to right; three uprights, the third nearer to the second than the first; a stroke curving to right; an upright; the extreme end of a stroke apparently descending from left; an upright turning out slightly to left 3 .[, ν possible though slightly anomalous; or perhaps two letters

Fr. 38

]επαν[
]τοιcε[
]αναξ[
]..ενεμ[

Fr. 38 4].., a dot, level with the top of the letters, close to the top of a circle

Fr. 39

```
.    .    .
        ].[
     ].ιδην[
     ]νιδα.[
      ].[]..[
   .    .    .
```

Fr. 39 1 A dot presumably the end of an upright descending below the line　2]., a dot level with the top of the letters　3 .[, o or c 4].[, the extreme top of a loop or circle　　]..[, the upper parts of two uprights, perhaps separate letters, followed by the left-hand end of a cross-stroke level with the top of the letters

2816. Hexameters (Cosmogony)

The imitations and reminiscences of early epic, especially Hesiod, in the invocation of the Muses which occupies ll. 1–8 of the following piece, suggest that it is the work of an archaizer, and this assumption is confirmed by the appearance in its vocabulary of words not recorded until they occur in Hellenistic verse. How much later than this it may be I am not competent to guess. Hexameters about the creation continued to be written for many centuries.

The text is written in an angular hand, a poor specimen of a common type, without lection signs. I should have supposed it might be dated in the second half of the second century, but it is on the back of a draft (of a letter?) in a bookhand with a heading in a cursive, both of which look to me certainly later than A.D. 200.

NEW CLASSICAL FRAGMENTS

Fr. 1

(a)   (c)

μουcαιπειεριδεcκουραιδιοcυψιμεδοντ[   ]   [

αιτεθεωνγενεcι.τεκαιαγλααδωρạ[   ]   [

πατροcεριcθενεοcχρυcεονπροcολ[   ].   [

πειεριηθεναπορνυμεναιορεοcζαθ[(b)   ]   [

5   ηετανυπρειωνοcαπεc .[ ].. [ ].[ ]λι.[   ]   [

ηεραεccαμεναιλι.[   ]οιδη[ ]   [

αυταιμοιμελπον[   ]ατε[ ]ολπην   [

ηεριαιπρομολου[   ]εραθ[ ] ον   [

               λι

ευτεπατηρλε[[ν]].[   ]απει[ ]ονακοcμον[

10   τευχεμενα.παιδε...[   ].cιον[ ]ομον αιει [

τημοcτεχνηεντινοω .[   ]ετοδ[ ]μων   [

εμμελεωc·ϊναπαcινεοι[   ].απει[ ]αθειη [

δειδιεγαρμη.εικοcενα [   ]ηλοιcι[ ]ντεc   [

ạιθεροcα[ ].τοιομε.[   ]..ιαπ[ ]τοcαια [

15   ηδεκαια.λ..οιcπελαγ[   ]εγα[ ]μαcιθυϊ[

εcχαοcανθιμ[ ]καιεc.[   ]ọνω.[ ]εcηcι [

τουνεκεν [ ]πρωτα[   ]..ρ.[ ]ϝετοτ[

                  ].

τονμεναρ[   ]ε.γε.[   ]..[

.   .   .   .

Fr. 2

].[

].α[

].χε[

]ετ[

.   .

Fr. 1 3]., the upper part of a slightly forward-sloping stroke   4 ορεοc ε ex ο *curr. cal.*   5 ει ex ω *curr. cal.*   In writing ç[υμ]ε̣ν[α]ι̣ I am by no means sure that I have correctly assigned the letters to the remaining ink   6 .[, the lower part of an upright; γ acceptable, but not uniquely 10 ...[, traces on the line, the first and third only dots, the middle compatible with the base of c   Of]ạ only the end of the tail   11 τη η written on a different letter, ? ω   .[, the foot of an upright 12 ι originally another letter, of which a projection, touching ν, remains   Of]τ only the right-hand end of the cross-stroke   14]., a faint trace, about mid letter, of the end of a stroke descending from left   .[, traces to right of the end of the cross-stroke of ε   Of]κ a faint dot presumably representing

Μοῦcαι Πιερίδεc, κοῦραι Διὸc ὑψιμέδοντ[οc,
αἵτε θεῶν γένεcίν τε καὶ ἀγλαὰ δῶρα[
πατρὸc ἐριcθενέοc χρύcεον πρὸc Ὀλ[υμπ-   ].
Πιερίηθεν ἀπορνύμεναι, ὄρεοc ζαθ[έοιο,

5   ἠὲ τανυπρήωνοc ἀπεcc[ύμ]ε̣ν̣[α]ι̣ ['Ε]λικ[ῶνοc,
ἠέρα ἐccάμεναι λιγ[ἀ]οιδη[
αὐταί μοι μέλπον[τι   ]ατε [μ]ολπήν
ἠέριαι προμολοῦ[cαι   ]ερα θ[.]ον.
εὖτε πατὴρ λελίη[-   ]ἀπεί[ρ]ονα κόcμον

10 τευχέμεναι παίδεcc.[   ]αcιον [.]ομον αἰεί,
τῆμοc τεχνήεντι νόωι .[   ]ετο δ[αί]μων
ἐμμελέωc, ἵνα πᾶcιν ἐοι[κό]τα πεί[ρατ]α θείη.
δείδιε γὰρ μὴ νεῖκοc ἐν ἀ[λλ]ήλοιcι [....]ν̣τεc
αἰθέροc ἀ[...].τοιο μέγ[οc]κ̣αὶ ἀπ[είρι]τοc αἶα

15 ἠδὲ καὶ ἀπλήτοιc πέλαγ[οc μ]έγα [κύ]μαcι θυῖον
ἐc Χάοc αὖθι μ[   ] καὶ εc.[   ]ονω.[π]έcηιcι.
τούνεκεν.[   ]πρωτα[   ]..ρ.[ ]ν̣ετοτ[
τὸν μὲν αρ[

- - - - - - - - - -

the tip of the upper arm   15 η is anomalous in having a cross-stroke carried through the
left-hand upright. Perhaps it was cancelled (and α superscribed)   16 χα α written on another
letter (or part of a letter)   c.[, a dot level with the top of c, and the foot of a stroke below and to right
on the line   ω.[, an upright of which the foot seems to be turning to right   17].., the top of
a tall upright, followed by a dot level with the top of the letters and on the line below it a nearly flat
stroke. I cannot rule out a single η   .[, c looks likeliest, but anomalous; perhaps an angular ο   ]ν
does not account for all the ink. The only alternative seems to be]λλ, but I doubt whether this is
acceptable   τ[is below the general level, but I see no alternative   18 I am not sure that]ε̣χ̣
should not be written, the cross-stroke between them being taken as the right-hand end of the cross-
stroke of ε   Above the line the lower end of a stroke curving down from left and touching the foot of
a slightly convex upright, hooked to right at the top   ]..[, the upper part of an upright with the tip of
a stroke rising from left against its top, followed by the apex of a triangular letter

Fr. 2 I am confident that this scrap is to be inserted into the left-hand part of fr. 1, 16 seqq., but
I am not sure that in ll. 16 seq. it actually touches as the facsimile makes it appear to do

1 A dot on the line   2]., the lower part of an upright   3 The same size as the other
lines but, if I am right about the location of the scrap, interlinear   ]., apparently the extreme lower
end of a stroke descending from left

1 Μοῦcαι Πιερίδεc: prima facie the beginning of the poem and to be compared with Hes. *Op.* 1
Μοῦcαι Πιερίηθεν. ἐξῆρχον ἀοιδῆc Μοῦcαι Πιερίδεc also at *Scut.* 206, but the common form of reference is
Μοῦcαι Ὀλυμπιάδεc (to which at *Theog.* 52 is added τὰc ἐν Πιερίηι . . . τέκε . . . Μνημοcύνη).

κοῦραι Διὸς ὑψιμέδοντος: common form is κ. Δ. αἰγιόχοιο. Hesiod has ὑψιμέδων in other phrases, *Theog.* 529, fr. 156, but the nearest to what is found here is Διὸς ὑψιμέδοντος παρθένοι . . . Πιερίδες Bacchyl. i 1 seq.

2 αἶτε where is the finite verb? Perhaps not till l. 6.

θεῶν γένεσιν: γένεσιν . . . θεῶν Aristoph. *Av.* 691. The word γένεσις not in Hesiod; in Homer in the locution Ὠκεανόν . . . θεῶν γένεσιν, *Il.* xiv 201, 302 (similarly ὅσπερ γένεσις πάντεσσι τέτυκται, l. 246), which is not comparable.

θεῶν . . . δῶρα: benefits flowing from the gods. Cf. *Theog.* 43 seqq.

κλέω and κλέομαι are not found in early epic, only κλείω, but that may not be a reason for denying this writer the possibility of κλέουσαι or κλέεσθε at the end of this verse.

3 πατρὸς ἐρισθενέος: *Il.* xix 355, *Od.* viii 289, Ζηνὸς ἐ. Hes. *Op.* 416.

Since χρύσεον cannot qualify Ὀλ[υμπον and πατρός requires prima facie a noun on which it depends, I suggest for want of anything better πρὸς Ὀλύμπιον οἶκον. I cannot justify οἶκον by any parallel from Homer or Hesiod, the earliest example (if it is an example) of Διὸς οἶκος I have found being Simon. **519** fr. 41 (a) 4. Cf. Eur. *Hipp.* 69 Ζηνὸς πολύχρυσον οἶκον, Callim. *hy.* iii 141 ἐς Διὸς οἶκον.

4 Cf. ἔνθεν (sc. Ἑλικῶνος) ἀπορνύμεναι Hes. *Theog.* 9, ἀπορνύμενον Λυκίηθεν *Il.* v 105.

ὄρος ζάθεον: h. Hom. Apoll. 223, ὅ. μέγα τε ζάθεόν τε *Theog.* 2.

5 τανυπρήων new; -πρι- for -πρη- in πολυπριωνα, Hermesian. (ap. Athen.) fr. 6, 57 P.

ἀπεσσύμεναι: I have not found the participle before Bacchylides, ἔνθεν (sc. Ἄργεος) ἀπεσσύμεναι xi 82. ἀπέσσυτο δώματος *Il.* vi 390.

6 ἠέρα ἐσσάμεναι cf. *Op.* 255 (-νοι), 223 (-νη), *Il.* xiv 282 (-νω). The equivalent at *Theog.* 9, of the Heliconian Muses, is κεκαλυμμέναι ἠέρι πολλῆι.

Prima facie probable comparisons are λιγυρήν, -ῆς, . . . ἀοιδήν, -ῆς, Hes. *Op.* 583, 659. If the verb of the relative clause was held up till this, possibilities suggested by *Il.* xviii 605, *Od.* xii 183, *Scut.* 205 are ἐντύνειν, ἐξάρχειν. A comma will be requisite at the end of the verse.

7 E.g. ἐμπνεύς]ατε cf. *Theog.* 31 ἐνέπνευσαν (sc. Μοῦσαι) δέ μοι αὐδήν (μ᾿ ἀοιδήν ci. Rzach, propter Aristid. cod. U μοι ἀοιδήν et Lucian. ὠιδήν).

8 ἠέριαι I suppose 'high up' as at *Il.* iii 7 of the cranes, which are οὐρανόθι πρό.

At the end of the line ἀνέρα θεῖον seems indicated. In case ἠ-, αἰθ-]έρα θεῖον is thought of, it should be said that the only example I can find of θεῖος in these phrases is as a variant in the quotation from Empedocles in Aristot. *de anim.* 404ᵇ8, *Metaph.* 1000ᵇ5, the regular usage in all kinds of writing being δῖ -ος, -α, *Il.* xvi 365, *Od.* xix 540, h. Hom. Dem. 70, Hes. *Theog.* 697, Aesch. *P.V.* 88, Q. Smyrn. xiii 464, Epig. gr. Kaibel 462, 13.

9 πατήρ by itself for Zeus e.g. at *Il.* viii 69, but a complement may have been lost in the gap.

λελίη[το, -τ᾿, -θ᾿. The finite verb first in Apollonius Rhodius, who has three examples of this form, followed as here by an infinitive. Earlier writers use only the participle as 'eagerly, vehemently' or the like.

ἀπείρονα κόσμον on the model of ἀπείρονα γαῖαν *Il.* vii 446, *Od.* xvii 418, *Theog.* 187, *Op.* 160, 487. From what follows the words appear to mean 'the world with unseparated constituents', but perhaps the writer thought of nothing more precise than 'vast'.

10 παίδεσσι, -σ᾿: though Zeus is πατὴρ ἀνδρῶν τε θεῶν τε, I have no passage (unless Aratus *Phaen.* 5) to adduce where these are called his children.

I suppose ἀσπ]άσιον is likely. ἀκηράσιον may be a possible alternative. Apart from these I believe there is effectively no choice. (A verbal resemblance to the first in *Od.* v 394, xi 431, ἀσπάσιος παίδεσσι.)

[δ]όμον suggests itself, but [ν]ομόν may not be ruled out. The general sense of ll. 9 seq. is presumably 'when the Father wished to make a place for his children in the universe . . .'. This implies the supplement κατ᾿ before ἀπείρονα. Further, the presence of αἰεί suggests, if it does not demand, the supplement ἔμεν before ἀσπ]άσιον; the construction as at *Il.* xviii 373 seq. τρίποδας . . . ἔτευχεν ἑστάμεναι περὶ τοῖχον.

12 'Set their proper bounds to all things', divide the universe into well-marked constituent parts. ἐοικότα 'seemly, suitable', e.g. *Od.* i 46 ἐοικότι κεῖται ὀλέθρωι, Ap. Rhod. *Argon.* iii 594 ἐοικότα μείλια τείσειν, Pind. *Isth.* v 24 κόμπον τὸν ἐοικότα.

πείρατα εἰ δύο εἴη . . . ἔχοι ἂν πείρατα πρὸς ἄλληλα, Melissus ap. Simplic. *de caelo* 557, 14.

13 E.g. τιθέ]ντες cf. *Od.* iii 136, *Il.* iv 83.

-τες is doubly peculiar, as masculine in apposition with two neuters and a feminine, as a hanging nominative with no finite verb. A simple correction of the second anomaly appears to be πέςωςι, l. 16, but in view of the uncertainty about the middle of that verse it may be illusory.

14 αἰθέρος . . . μένος for this periphrasis cf. Emped. fr. 115, 9 αἰθέριον . . . μένος, and even, it seems, αἴης λάςιον μένος (γένος Plut., em. Bergk) id. fr. 27, 2.

ἁ[. . .].τοιο the exiguous trace before τ does not appear to me to suggest either ε or α. I think it is compatible with ς.

ἀπείριτος αἶα: cf. Hes. *Theog.* 878 γαῖαν ἀπείριτον.

15 ἄπλητος not Homeric, in *Theog.* and *Scut.* and later writers, often with variants -πλα- and -πλας-, meaning vaguely 'fearsome'.

πέλαγος μέγα *Il.* xiv 16 (where κύματι κωφῶι follows), *Od.* iii 179, 321.

πέλαγος . . . οἴδματι θυῖον *Theog.* 131, οἴδματι θυίων (sc. πόντος) *Il.* xxiii 230, *Theog.* 109. At **2322** fr. 1, 17 seq. (Anacreon?) θυίοντα . . . κύμαςι the diphthong is written, as here, with a *trema*, but is scanned as short.

16 αὖθι for αὖθις a Hellenistic use.

ὦκ[α appears to be possible.

2817. Poem in Hexameters

In the little that I can decipher with certainty of the following column there are recognizable references to hunting and to the south-eastern end of the Propontis. The hunting is done, at any rate in part, by a woman, and there is a reasonable chance that her name is given in l. 20. The love-story of Arganthone, whose home was Kius or thereabouts, and Rhesus is recorded by Parthenius (π. ἐρωτικῶν παθημάτων xxxvi), whose prose version is presumed to be an abstract of an Alexandrian poem. Whether these rags of verse might represent it I see nothing to show and I have found no clue to the identity of the author.[1]

The verses are written on the back of a late 1st/2nd century cursive document, of which only a few letters remain, in a commonplace upright bookhand without lection signs. I suppose it may be assigned to a date about the middle of the second century. Owing to fraying and warping it is in many places difficult to be certain of the exact relation to one another of the surviving traces.

```
      ]μαccαγετηνατρακτονο[
      ]χερc[ . ]νεπειγομενηιcιβ[
      ]  αιψαδεκυκλωθητανᾱον[
      ]δυcκελαδουπωγωγᾱαπ[
  5   ]πηξεδυποκρᾳδιηνολοογ[
      ]νυμφαιμακροναυcαν[ ] . [
      ]καιτριχαcεξ . . αμον . []κ . [
      ]και . . μενυ . . νε . ε . . [ ] . ο . . [
      αιει . ηραcεν . [ . ] . ενᾳ[   ]χε . [
 10   ευτε[ . ]εθερμ[   ] . [ ] . [   ] . c . . [] . [
      αζαλεηιcοδυ[ ] . . [   ]μεͅ . [] . μα . [
      κρηνηcλευκ[ . . ]ε . [     ] . ρηγ . . [
      παρθενοcαφρ[ . . ]το[   ]μουκη[]υ[
      ουδεμεναγρ[ . ]τη[       ] . αιπολο[
 15   . ηρωcκαιευ . [] . τα[] . . . [] . αλιcͅ[ ] . . [
      γηνμε . επελ[] . εβ . . υ . ανολον βρηνα . . [
       . δ[ . ]ακͅεcαιcηπο[ . ]ο . . [ . . . . ]νιουπ[ . ]ριπηχυ[
      θηλυκο[ . . . ]βρε . [ . ]αιε . [ . . ] . νδοροc . . ρονᾳ[
      μυγδοͅν[   ] . ιοε . . ε . κ . [   ] . αργανθω . . [
 20   εξαγρηcαγιου[ . ]ᾳνεδε[ . ]κεοπυκναδε . [
      μαιναδοcαγρω[ . ]ταιcινεπϊυζωνcκυ[
```

<hr/>

[1] If in l. 19 nothing but μυ[. .]ον[—]αργανθωνη[had survived, Simylus (Bergk *PLG* iii p. 515) might have raised hopes with a false trail.

5 Of ν[only a speck on a single fibre   6].[, the lower part of an upright descending below the line   7 After ξ traces compatible with ε but by no means suggesting it, followed by the right-hand end of a cross-stroke as of γ   ν.[, a cross-stroke level with the top of the letters   κ.[the lower part of an upright?   8 After ι the left-hand arc of a small circle, before μ the upper part of an upright branching to right; cυ?   Between υ and ν (of which the right-hand upright), on separate fibres, the upper end of a stroke descending to right and having traces on its left; a small hook, open to right, on the line; an upright, perhaps the left-hand stroke of ν   ε..[, the tip of an upright, followed at an interval by the upper part of a thin upright turning over to right at the top   ]., a dot above the top of the letters   ..[, an upright descending well below the line, followed by another shorter   9 Between ι and η a trace on the line   .[, indeterminate traces   ]., the right-hand arc of a small circle at mid letter   .[, an upright trending to right at its foot   10 ..[, the right-hand end of a thin cross-stroke about mid letter, followed by an upright; a single η might be possible   11 After ι a dot to right of its top   12 .[, the left-hand end of a cross-stroke level with the top of the letters and below it a short upright on the line   ].., scattered traces, the first perhaps the lower end of a stroke descending from left, the last the right-hand end of a cross-stroke at mid letter   ..[, a dot on the line, followed by the start of a stroke rising to right   14]., a slightly convex upright   15 Before η opposite ends of a cross-stroke off the line   .[]., an upright with a thickened top, followed by the right-hand end of a cross-stroke with a trace below; perhaps no whole letter missing   ]...[, on a narrow strip the lower ends of two strokes suggesting λ or the like, followed by the left-hand side of a small circle, and this by a dot and a hook to right on the line   ]..[, perhaps the overhang and end of the turn-up of c, followed by an upright with traces to right   16 Of ε only the left-hand curve; followed by the feet of two uprights, close together, nearer ε   After β on a single fibre two diverging strokes suggesting the upper part of the loop of α; before υ the foot of an upright having to its right the lower end of a stroke descending from left. Between this and υ interlinear ink   After υ the lower part of an upright; the spacing suggests τ   ..[, the foot of an upright below the line, followed by a trace compatible with the left-hand side of a small circle   17 The first letter unverifiable; ε not suggested   ..[, a speck off the line, followed by the right-hand part of a small circle off the line   Below ο[ι]ο a small hook open to right, followed by the end of a stroke rising from left; possibly relate to the letters below, αι l. 18   18 ρε.[, the foot of an upright hooked to right   ε.[, the middle part of a stroke rising from left, followed by a dot about level with its upper end   ]., the top of an upright   Between c and ρ faint specks   19]., the right-hand part of a cross-stroke as of γ   Between ε and ϛ an upright closely followed by the left-hand end of a cross-stroke level with its top, and this by a speck about mid letter   Before κ the upper right-hand side of a small circle; o or ρ suggested   .[, on the line a hook open to right?   ]., the foot of an upright and the lower end of a diverging stroke a little higher to right   ..[, feet of three strokes; no doubt ν, and perhaps ι or η   20 .[, an upright

1 For Μασσαγέται as archers cf. Callim. fr. 1, 15 with Pfeiffer's references there. Μασσαγέτης adjectival in Nonn. *Dionys.* xl. 287 M. παρὰ κόλπον, Agathias *Anth. Pal.* iv 3ᵇ 32 seq. M. δέ | ἀμφιθέων ἀγκῶνα.

ἄτρακτος 'spindle', for 'arrow'. Aesch. fr. 139 (*Myrmid.*) ἀτράκτωι τοξικῶι, Eur. *Rhes.* 312 ἀτράκτων τοξόται.

As the geographical names in the lower part of the column refer to the parts of Mysia south of the eastern end of the Propontis, it looks as if Μασσαγέτην was ornamental.

2 χερσὶν ἐπειγομένηισι: I can find no satisfactory parallel to this form of phrase before Nonn. *Dionys.* xxix 103 φειδομέναις παλάμηισι. ἐπειγομένων ἀνέμων *Il.* v 501 and ὧραι ἐπειγόμεναι Pind. *Nem.* iv 34 do not seem to me comparable.

β[: in the context some case of βιός may be thought of. Reasonable guesses at the contents of the lost parts of vv. 1 seq. might be based on, e.g., *Il.* iv 116 σύλα πῶμα φαρέτρης ἐκ δ' ἕλετ' ἰόν, viii 323 φαρέτρης ἐξείλετο πικρὸν ὀιστόν and iv 118 ἐπὶ νευρῆι κατεκόσμεε πικρὸν ὀιστόν, viii 324 θῆκε δ' ἐπὶ νευρῆι. Cf. Ap. Rhod. *Argon.* iii. 278 seqq.

3 αἶψα δ' ἐκυκλώθη ταναὸν [κέρας? Cf. Eur. *Bacch.* 1066 κυκλοῦτο δ' ὥστε τόξον (*Il.* iv 124 κυκλοτερὲς μέγα τόξον ἔτεινε).

κέρας for 'bow', not Homeric (except that some saw it in κέραι ἀγλαέ *Il.* xi 385), but Callim. *Epig.* 37, 3 seq. κέρας... καὶ φαρέτρην, [Theoc.] xxv 206 κέρας ὑγρὸν... κοίλην τε φαρέτρην, corresponding to

Homeric τόξον . . . φαρέτρην (*Il.* i 45, xv 443, *Od.* xxi 59), βιὸν . . . φαρέτρην (*Il.* x 260, *Od.* xxi 233, xxii 2), simm.

3 seq. δυσκελάδου and πώγων imply a mention of 'arrow'. πώγωνες—I have found the singular nowhere but here—are the barbs, Pollux vii 158 βέλους δ' αἱ ἀκίδες ὄγκοι (the Homeric word, *Il.* iv 151) καὶ πώγωνες καλοῦνται; cf. Hesych. in ὄγκοι, ὄγκους, Schol. A *Il.* l.c. They may have been mentioned here in a description of drawing the arrow to the head, as in *Il.* iv 123 νευρὴν μὲν μαζῶι πέλασεν τόξωι δὲ σίδηρον.

δυσκελάδου: I have not found elsewhere of arrows, the nearest being δυσηχέας . . . ὀιστούς Ap. Rhod. *Argon.* iii 96 (also unique?).

5 πῆξε δ' ὑπὸ κραδίην ὀλοὸν [βέλος: cf., e.g., *Od.* xxii 83 ἐν δέ οἱ ἥπατι πῆξε θοὸν βέλος. For ὑπό with accusative in place of ἐν (usual in phrases of this type) cf., e.g., Soph. *Antig.* 1315 παίσας' ὑφ' ἧπαρ . . . αὐτήν, *Trach.* 931 ὑφ' ἧπαρ καὶ φρένας πεπληγμένην.

6 νύμφαι or Νύμφαι?

μακρὸν ἄυσαν: besides Homer cf. Callim. fr. 260, 4. At Theocr. iv 35 seqq. μ. ἀνάυσαν of women. If the interpretation of the next verse is correct, a cry of triumph.

7 καὶ τρίχας ἐξέταμον (or -οντ[) can hardly be avoided. I suppose the reference is to a ritualistic act similar to those described at *Il.* iii 273, xix 254, *Od.* iii 446, xiv 422 seq., Eur. *El.* 811 seq., though I cannot recognize any other implication that this is a solemn occasion.

9 αἰεὶ θῆρας ἔναιρ- not verifiable but suggested by the recurrence of θῆρας ἔναιρ- in various places, *Il.* xxi 485, *h. Hom.* v 18, xix 13, Eur. *Hipp.* 1129, (Soph. *Phil.* 956). ἔναιρε is an imperfect at Pind. *Nem.* iii 47, Q. Smyrn. i 395, Eur. l.c. (ex corr.), but in view of the apparent presence of σύ in l. 8 and the occurrence of second persons in ll. 17 and 20, it is necessary to consider the possibility that it is an imperative here.

11 ἀζαλέηις' ὀδύνηισι 'drouthy pains', cf. διψαλέην ὀδύνην epig. ap. Luc. *Dips.* 6 and perhaps αὐχμηραὶ νόσοι Emped. 121, 3.

14 More than one articulation possible. If οὐδὲ μέν cf. *Il.* xii 82, Hes. *Op.* 785, Xenophan. fr. 2, 17.

Apparently not enough room for [ως], too much for [ι]. In the neighbourhood of αἰπολο- some form of ἀγρώτης or ἀγρώτηρ (cf. Soph. *Ichn.* 1174 ii 6 εἴτε ποι]μὴν εἴτ' ἀγρωτή[ρων τις) looks acceptable. But there are other possibilities.

15 It does not look as if the first letter could be anything but ψ, though there is no other example for comparison. ψηρῶς, equivalent to ξηρῶς, has not a strong backing, but I can think of no substitute as likely.

16 βρηναι.[: no Greek word, whether common noun or proper name, begins, so far as I can discover, with these letters.

17 ἔδρακες Αἰσήποιο . . . The river Aesepus, the Mygdonian country, the Arganthonian height are encountered by one proceeding from west to east on the south coast of the Propontis. If there is anything in the hypothesis set out below (l. 19, note), for 'Arganthonian height' may be substituted Kius.

περὶ πῆχυν: parts of the body are freely used in reference to topographical features (see e.g. αὐχήν, ἀγκών, λαγών, λόφος, νῶτον, ὀφρῦς, πούς, σφυρόν, τένων, χεῖλος), but I cannot find that πῆχυς is so used and it is hard to see to what it could apply.

19 Μυγδον- Mygdonians are reported in widely separated areas of the Greek world. Here I suppose the name refers to the countryside or people described by Strabo xii 575 as north of the Mysian Olympus and extending as far as the territory of Myrlea.

Ἀργανθων-: both -νι[(as e.g. Ἀργανθώνιον αἶπος Euphor. 75 P) and -νη[are compatible with a reference to the mountain above Kius, but in view of ἐξ ἄγρης ἀνιοῦσαν in the next line there is reasonable ground for conjecturing that in Ἀργανθώνη[ν] is to be recognized the heroine of the story related by Parthenius (*Narr. Amat.* xxxvi) and alluded to by Stephanus in Ἀργανθών and Eustathius (Arrian.) on Dionys. περ. 322 and 809.

20 ἐξ ἄγρης ἀνιοῦσαν ἐδέρκεο after the model of ἐκ πομπῆς ἀνιοῦσαν *Od.* viii 568, xiii 150, 176, but I have found elsewhere only ἄγρης (ex corr.) ἐξανιών *h. Hom.* xix 15, θήρης ἐξανιών Ap. Rhod. *Argon.* iii 69 (ἐξ ἀνιών Fränkel).

20 seq. πυκνὰ δε.[| μαινάδος ἀγρώσταισιν ἐπιύζων σκυλάκεσσι. At first sight δὲ κούρης would be suitable. It would apparently necessitate the assumption that a verb parallel to ἐδέρκεο occurred

subsequently. But μαινάδοc could stand by itself and δ' ἐ.[is consistent with the required tense of a verb. Or again it is possible that δε.[does not contain δέ.

ἀγρῶcται· οἱ κυνηγοί schol. Ap. Rhod. *Argon.* iv 175. I have no example of the adjectival use in this sense. Cf. κύνες ἀγρευταί Solon 23, ἀγρευτῆρcι κύνεccι Oppian. *Cyn.* iii 456.

cκύλακεc of the hounds of Actaeon Eur. *Bacch.* 338, of Artemis Callim. *hy.* iii 87.

ἐπΐύζων: this compound not attested.

2818. Hexameters

Of the composition represented by the following remnants of hexameter verses not enough is left for me to make a guess at its subject or the identity of its author. To judge by appearances the scrap comes from a roll of quite high quality, but the performance of a copyist is no guide to the literary value of his text.

The text is written in a good-sized, well-spaced uncial, comparable with **1090, 1806** and others, assigned to the end of the first century. The only addition to the bare letters is a high stop, l. 11.

```
              .         .          .
      ].ηcεκ[..]ειμακ[
      ]μενηcβαcιλη[
      ]ενηγαρεπ[
      ].:.εκαιαδρη[
 5    ]ωνεπιηραν.[
      ]πο[
      ]ρηαδαϊζομενων.....[
      ]αγονεccικαιαιπεινουκαc[
      ]ααcεκατονταδαcειλιποδ[
10    ]φαιcτοιομυρειναιηπαραβα[
      ]ψαcακαλαcφλογαc·αρεαλοι[
      ]ολιπορθοναδηρειτ.υπα[
```

1]., an upright   4]..., of the first letter the right-hand end of a horizontal stroke on the line and faint specks above to right; the second letter presumably ι (υ ruled out) but not recognizable; the third represented by the upper ends of two converging strokes, the right-hand the longer, and below them on the line the left-hand end of a horizontal stroke   7 Of]ρ only the lower part, ε perhaps possible   .....[, the base of a circle, followed by the lower parts of three uprights, then the lower part of an upright with the right-hand end of a cross-stroke to right, level with the top of the letters, then the top and base of a circle; επι followed by γ or τ and ε or ο suggested   10 Of]φ only part of the right-hand loop   11 Of]ψ only the upper part of the upright   12 Of]ρ only the upper right-hand curve   Between τ and υ presumably the bottom left-hand curve of ο, but below this letter is the left-hand end of a stroke rising slightly to right

4 As ϊ does not appear to be preceded by a vowel, ἴζε or ἴξε is the only choice.

As a curiosity I mention Antim. fr. 53, 4 τετίμηταί τε καὶ Ἀδρήcτεια καλεῖται. I should guess that some form of Ἀδρήcτεια was not improbable in l. 4, whether as a geographical term (v. P–W in v.), like those in ll. 8 and 10, or as a reference to Nemesis (v. Wyss ad Antim. l.c., Pfeiffer ad Callim. fr. 299).

5 It is possible to divide]ων ἐπίηρα ν.[and take -ων either as a participle, φέρων, or a genitive plural after ἐπίηρα, or, as I think much more likely,]ων ἐπιήρανος (in some form), the genitive after ἐπιήρανος in one of its senses. There are more distant possibilities, e.g. γέρ]ων.

8 λ]αγόνεσσι: cf. Βριλησσοῦ λαγόνεσσι Callim. fr. 552.

αἰπεινοῦ Κασ[ίοιο. There are two mounts Kasius, one in Egypt (θινώδης τις λόφος ἀκρωτηριάζων Strabo xvi 2, 33) near Pelusium, the other in Syria, not far from the mouth of the Orontes, qualified as βαθύκρημνος by Dionysius (περιηγ. l. 880).

9 κερ]αὰς . . . εἰλίποδ[ας βοῦς: κεραῶν . . . βοῶν Callim. fr. 23, 1 fr. 67, 10; εἰλίποδας βοῦς Il. xv 547.

10 ῾Ηφαίστοιο Μυριναίη: apparently an allusion to Lemnos with its two towns ῾Ηφαιστία (St. Byz. in v., or ῾Ηφαίστεια schol. Callim. fr. 384 ll. 25 seq.) and Μύρινα.

11 Perhaps ἅ]ψασα καλὰς φλόγας, but ἀκαλὰς φλόγας may not be an impossible combination. ἅπτειν πῦρ e.g. Eur. *Hel.* 503 (but ἐρείκης θῶμον ἅψαντες πυρί Aesch. *Agam.* 295). The plural of φλόξ does not seem to occur before Aristotle. In verse Nicand. *Georg.* fr. 74, 48, Orph. *Lith.* 173.

11 seq. Ἄρεα . . . πτολίπορθον cf. Ἄρηα πτολίπορθον Il. xx 152. But Ἄρεα is an uncommon form for which I can only adduce Ap. Rhod. *Argon.* i 1024 Πελασγικὸν Ἄρεα.

12 ἀδήριτον 'irresistible', Aesch. *P.V.* 105.

2819. Commentary on a Hexameter Poem

It is not unreasonable to conjecture that the poem, of which the following fragments of a commentary on it preserve a few words and phrases, was at least in part concerned with the route followed by Io. The occurrence of Io is deducible from the mention of Epaphus in fr. 1 (which may also contain references to what is called in the *Prometheus* πόντιος μυχὸς . . . Ἰόνιος and to a Βόσπορος). It is, therefore, not far-fetched to see in fr. 2 a specification of the stage in her journey corresponding to *Prometheus* 830 seq. ἵνα μαντεῖα θᾶκός τ' ἐςτὶ Θεςπρωτοῦ Διός, and, again, in fr. 4 a fixing by means of the Symplegades of the Thracian (as e.g. Apollod. *Bibl.* ii 1, 3 5, not as *Prometheus* 729 seqq. the Cimmerian) Bosporus as the place where she crossed from Europe to Asia.

A distant possibility of a clue to the authorship may occur in fr. 2.

The commentary itself is of the usual sort and has at first sight a very simple layout. A word or short piece of the poetic text, lemma, is followed by a short explanation and this by another lemma. A blank space, equivalent to about two letters, is left between lemma and comment and between comment and lemma. There is no other articulation, in particular no ἔκθεςις. But from place to place this description is inapplicable. In fr. 11, 2 seq., for example, the writing is not continuous, but the right-hand part of the lines is left blank; and similarly at fr. 2, 9 and 16, fr. 4, 17.

The text is written in an elegant small bookhand which I suppose may be dated early in the second century. The ink, though I do not think it is metallic, has faded and worn. There appear to be signs that repairs of one sort and another had already become necessary in antiquity.

Fr. 1

(*a*)   .   .   .

].τοιϲϲυμβ[

].ετ.ψ[

]   [

]επαφονοτιεπη[

5   ]νομαϲθ..η.ηλ.[

].νιωγαιηϲπ.[.]η [

]αναποπλαϲ[.]ο.[]ε [

]αλλαβ.ϲ[]..[

]ευϲε[]   [

10   ].εχ.[.].η[.]αν[

].[ ]χρω[

]....ωϲνν.[

]α..ιϲοϲϲη.[   ].[

]..ιπαιδι[..]ωραι[

15   ]ιαμονοϲα[.]δροϲ [

].φροϲυνηιαλλα   [

]ιϲαιπαϲαι   [

].οϲπαμπη[

]   [

20   ].ουαρϲ[(*b*) .   .   .

]ιδα [   ]παντελωϲ[

]πειν.[   ]εναι   [

]κακω[.   .   .

].ιϲφ.[

(*c*) .   .   .   (*d*) .   .   .

25   ]..[ ].[].[

]ηροϲτοτ[   ]ω.[

].εξαϲν[   ]ιδ'τον[

]ηαπν[   ]ιαϲβου.[

].α[   ].νηρ [

.   .   .   .   .   .

Fr. 1 The level and interval of (*b*) in relation to (*a*) are fixed by the fibres on either side. The position of (*c*) below (*a*) is established by the vertical fibres, but its distance is uncertain and may be considerable. The level of (*d*) in relation to (*c*) is fixed by the cross-fibres, but I cannot follow the vertical fibres of (*b*) into (*d*) and the interval between (*c*) and (*d*) is therefore not to be fixed with any precision. It cannot be very great, if the ends of the lines, 26–9, are to correspond more or less with the line-endings above

1 Of β[only the base   4 Of τ only the foot of the stalk   5 After θ perhaps the apex of α; θαι possible   .[, apparently the lower part of an upright, but the surface is disturbed   6]., a dot at mid letter   .[, a dot on the line   7 .[, the start of a stroke rising to right   8 Between β and ς an elongated dot at mid letter   ]..[, the upper end, hooked to left, of a stroke descending to right, closely followed by the upper left-hand arc of a small circle   10]., the upper part of an upright .[, perhaps η, but in a much damaged place   ]., the right-hand end of a cross-stroke level with the top of the letters   Of]α only the tail   12]., the foot of a stroke hooked to right, followed by dispersed traces   .[, a dot on the line   13 Between α and ι faint traces ending with the right-hand side of a circle   .[, the lower part of a stroke rising to right   ].[, a tall forward-sloping stroke 14 Before ιτ a short upright   16]., a short upright stroke at mid letter   18]., a dot level with the top of the letters   20]., the right-hand end of a cross-stroke touching the top of ο   22 .[, the left-hand side of a circle; ω likely   24]., very faint, perhaps the loop of ρ   .[, the ink, more than normally distant from φ, now resembles γ more than any other letter; perhaps ιτ, but I do not find this very convincing   25]..[, the bottom right-hand arc of a circle, followed by the foot of a stroke hooked-up to right, e.g. ϲ   26 .[, the foot of an upright   27]., against the top of ε the upper end of a stroke rising from left   Of ρ[only the left-hand side   28 For π perhaps γ. 29]., a short arc compatible with the loop of ρ   ]., a dot level with the top of the letters

Fr. 1 4 seq. Perhaps an etymologizing note. Ἔπαφον and ὠ]νομάϲθαι look fairly safe. ὅτι ἐπή[φηϲε is a long shot, but may render the presumed meaning; Ἔπαφοϲ ἐκλήθη, ἐπεὶ ὁ Ζεὺϲ ἐπαφηϲάμενοϲ τῆϲ Ἰοῦϲ πάλιν εἰϲ γυναῖκα αὐτὴν μετεμόρφωϲε Schol. Eur. *Phoen.* 678 (Aesch. *P.V.* 848 seqq.).

6 Ἰ]ονίω⟨ι⟩ cannot be verified, but has a reasonable appearance of likelihood in this context. The derivation from Ἰώ at Aesch. *P.V.* 839 seqq.

γαίηϲ part of a lemma or quotation.

7 seq. ἀποπλαϲ[ϲ]ομε|ν- seems unavoidable. The possibility occurred to me of ἀποπλαζομένη, spelt with -ϲδ- for -ζ-, as ἀοϲδεῖ in fr. 4, 4. This word would have had relevance to Io, but no other example of ἀποπλάζομαι is recorded in any tense but the aorist.

8 βοϲ[π]ορ[is an obvious guess. I cannot verify it.

15 -άμονοϲ ἀνδρόϲ looks probable and, if it is right, the preceding ι must be supposed, in spite of appearances, to represent π, since no adjective ends in -ιάμων and, if ι represented any other letter ending in an upright, not -α- but -η- would be required.

21 παντελῶϲ perhaps an interpretation of παμπή[δην, l. 18; cf. Hesych. in v., schol. Soph. *Aj.* 916.

22 τετα]πεινω[.]έναι?

Fr. 2

```
          ·                  ·
        ]αφε . . ιαμυν[
        ]ωιγενειπρος [
        ] . ιϲδ᾽τωναντιγρα [
        ]ϲεθνοϲειναι       [
   5    ] . υμενονφερε      [
        ] . ουλεγεταιδεφηϲιν[
        ]νειοντεϲηϲαν[
        ]ινωνομαϲμε[
        ]              [
   10   ]ϲλεγουϲι      [
        ] . αγ᾽ελεγετοη [
        ]αρατομετοι[
           ] . [ ]ονα[
           ] . . . [ ]εϲ    [
   15   ]εναζ[ . ]μ[ . ] . οιϲ [
        ]              [
        ] . ουε . αβ . . εν   [
        ] . . θ . . []α . . νιου [
          ·      ·       ·
```

Fr. 2 1 . ., a speck on the line, followed after a gap by faint traces to left of the top of ι   After ν no trace on the line but a suspended letter or ο would have been carried away   3]., traces compatible with ο, but not suggesting it   5]., a trace about mid letter   6]., the upper part of an upright   11]., the lower part of an upright descending well below the line   12 Of]α only the back but suggested by the spacing   13].[, ν seems acceptable   17]., the right-hand end of a cross-stroke touching the top of ο   Before α the lower end of a stroke descending from left   After β a crescent off the line, not suiting ε, ο, or ϲ of this hand, followed by what looks like the top of γ   18 Partly rewritten in blacker ink   ]. ., the right-hand end of a cross-stroke touching the top of ο? . .[, the top of an upright, the upper end of a stroke descending to right, the left-hand arc of a small circle at the same level; if three letters, rather cramped   For]α possibly λ   The last four letters except ο are very doubtful

Fr. 2 1 (-)γρ]άφεται.

1 seq. αμυν, if the end of the line, as seems likely, must be followed by a consonant. I suggest Ἀμύν|ται, or some case of it, for a reason which appears below, l. 7.

3 seq. ἐν ἐνί]οιϲ δὲ τῶν ἀντιγρά|φων.

4 Perhaps Θεϲπρωτία]ϲ, see l. 7.

5 seq. φέρε|ται 'is found in a text', 'recorded', simm.

7 I suggest π]νείοντεϲ. Steph. Byz. in Ἀμύνται has ἔθνοϲ Θεϲπρωτικόν, μένοϲ πνείοντεϲ Ἀμύνται . . ., which is conjectured to be a quotation of Rhianus (whose name appears in the previous article). If the same words occurred here, there is no telling whether they were lemma or quotation.

7 seq. ? ἦcαν . . . ὠνομαcμέ[νοι.
11 seq. ? -α γ(ὰρ) ἐλέγετο ἤ . . . παρὰ τὸ μετοι-, 'X was given the name -α from (because of) . . .'
15 (-)cκ]εναζ[ο]μ[έ]νοιc.

Fr. 3

Fr. 3 4 The first two letters are in black ink and might be ια, the third is in the usual brown and might be c represented by the top stroke   7 The count of letters is quite uncertain

Fr. 4

```
                 .   .   .   .        .    .    .    .    .    .    .
             ].. .[
        ]    εχουσααλλε[    ].ọ.    [
        ]   ∕ιϲτιοναμφ[   ].ν   γαλη[
        ]   ∕αοϲδει  λα.[  ]ọτιεγινετοδ[
   5    ]    πληγαδαπαρπετρην τηνϲυμ[
        ]    μενηνυποτ'νεωτερων  τη[.]δουκενιφυλ.[
           ]  ωνων  ωϲαορνουκαθεϲτωτ[.]ϲτουτοπου      [
           ]  αλλαυτωϲλειηπαραδεδρομεν  αλλωϲεχει       [
                  ]παρηκει  τεκτωννννντονοικοδο          [
   10           ].λατυποντεκτοναερρ⁊  ουδενιβ.          [
                ].κοπαιεφων...ητιϲενθειϲτονποδα         [
                ]ϲλειηπαραδε[.]ρομεν  μηπροϲπλη         [
                ]ειαεπιπολυνπαρηκειτοπον  κελα[
                ].ατουεπιθετọυτουδωρδηλοιọπουϲ          [
   15           ]αποιονηχονεντωιρεινκαιοποιητ⁊[
                ]τοδετωκακạτειβομενονκελαρυζει          [
                ].                                      [
                ].α  λ[.]υκαυνοιϲατοπελαγọϲλευκα        [
                ]....[ ].τω.αλευκαθεοιϲα               [
   20                      ].γ.[
                        stripped
                        ].     [
                        ]...[
                 .        .        .        .
```

Fr. 4 1].. ., the lower end of an upright descending below the line, followed by a speck on the line and a short horizontal stroke off the line   **2**].ọ., apparently]ṛọ or].ịọ, followed by the overhang of ϲ, but all the indications are very doubtful   **3**]., if one letter, η; if two, ι preceded by γ, τ, ψ suggested   **4** .[, a stroke rising to right; neither λ nor μ suggested   Of τ only the foot of the stalk and perhaps the left-hand end of the cross-stroke; not prima facie ν for τι   **10**]., a dot on the line   After β I think the base of the loop of α, but ο may not be ruled out   **11** Of]ϲ only the overhang, which is unusually extended   **12** μη, μ not satisfactory, but I see nothing else more likely   **14** ọπ, ọ is anomalous and further than expected from π, but I do not think α can be substituted   **18**]., a speck about mid letter   **19**]....[, the tops of an uncertain number of letters. The last is represented by the upper left-hand arc of a small circle, which is preceded by what looks like an apostrophe   ]., a cross-stroke level with the cross-stroke of τ   Between ω and α two uprights, presumably ν or π   **20**]., the upper part of α or λ   .[, the top of an upright   **23**]., δ or λ .[, perhaps the upper left-hand side of ϲ

Fr. 4 3 A case of γαλήνη or some derivative.

4 On ἄοζοϲ and ἀοζεῖν see Pfeiffer on Callim. fr. 563. In view of the interpretations 'servant', 'serve', and the like, I may as well remark that there is no chance that λατ[ρ- was written here.

```
     ·     ·     ·     ·     ·     ·     ·     ·     ·
     ]...[
     ἔχουϲα ἀλλ' ε[      ].ọ. [
     ἱϲτίον ἀμφ[   ].ν  γαλη[
     ἀοϲδεῖ  λα.[   ]οτι ἐγίνετο δ[
5    πληγάδα παρ πέτρην·  τὴν ϲυμ[πληγάδα λεγο-
     μένην ὑπὸ τ(ῶν) νεωτέρων. τῆ[ι] δ' οὐκ ἔνι φῦλ' ο[ἰ-
     ωνῶν·  ὡϲ ἀόρνου καθεϲτῶτ[ο]ϲ τοῦ τόπου.
     ἀλλ' αὔτωϲ λείη παραδέδρομεν·  ἀλλ' ὡϲ ἔχει
              ]παρήκει . τέκτων· νῦν τὸν οἰκοδό-
10   μον      ]. λατύπον τέκτονα εἴρη(κεν). οὐδενι β.-
              ]ϲκοπαί, ἐφ' ὧν βαίη τιϲ ἐνθεὶϲ τὸν πόδα,
     ἀλλ' αὔτω]ϲ λείη παραδέδρομεν. μὴ προϲπλη-
              ]εια ἐπὶ πολὺν παρήκει τόπον. κελα-
     ρυζ-     δ]ιὰ τοῦ ἐπιθέτου τὸ ὕδωρ δηλοῖ οπουϲ
15            ]α ποιὸν ἦχον ἐν τῶι ῥεῖν, καὶ ὁ ποιητή(ϲ)
              ]τὸ δέ τ' ὦκα κατειβόμενον κελαρύζει.
              ].
              ].α λ[ε]υκαίνουϲα τὸ πέλαγοϲ λευκϲ.
              ]....[].τω.α λευκαθέοιϲα
```

I cannot account for the eccentric dialectal spellings here and below at ll. 18 seq. ἀοϲϲεῖν (ἀοϲϲῆϲαι at Mosch. iv 110), which appears to have a similar meaning, I suppose to be extracted from ἀοϲϲητήρ and to have no relevance.

5 The singular Ϲυμπληγάϲ, which it must be assumed the commentator said was the name used by the νεώτεροι, is found only in two places in Euripides (*I.T.* 241, *Androm.* 794), in both of which it has been called in question. I suppose the commentator was referring only to the compound form and not to the number. Apollonius Rhodius, who uses the simple form like this poet, uses the plural, *Argon.* ii 596 Πληγάϲι, ii 644 seq. πέτραϲ Πληγάδαϲ, fr. 5, 4 P. A lone 'clasher' has a Dundreary flavour about it.

8 'It stretches all smooth alongside . . .' The use of παρατρέχειν in the sense of παρήκειν is not recorded in LSJ.

9 τέκτων perhaps to illustrate λείη, as smooth as if a builder or mason had made it.
νῦν, as commonly, 'in this place'.

10 ἐρρ- I suppose simply a mistake.

10 seq. ϲκοπαί (and ϲκοπιαί) are hilltops, which, since they are used for lookouts, can be walked on, ἐφ' ὧν βαίη τιϲ ⟨ἂν⟩ ἐνθεὶϲ τὸν πόδα. I suppose they are contrasted with the mountain being described, which offers no foothold. But I can make no convincing suggestion for the articulation or completion of οὐδενιβ..

13 λ]εία?

14 I should suppose the subject of δηλοῖ to be the poet, but I have no idea what is to be made of the end of the line.

15 On comparison with the phraseology of *Et.M.* in κελαρύζω one might expect ἀποτελοῦϲ]α ποιὸν ἦχον ἐν τῶι ῥεῖν or something not much different.

15 seq. Homer at *Il.* xxi 261.

18 seq. λ[ε]υκαννοιϲα the second υ appears to have been made out of ι, I suppose by mistake for the ι of the termination. The text had the dialectal spelling but there was no reason for the comment to retain it.

λευκαθέοιϲα (which I suppose to be a repetition of the lemma) is only the second example of the verb postulated for Hes. *Scut.* 146 ὀδόντων . . . λευκαθεόντων. A difficulty which I cannot resolve is that λευκαθέω (like the much commoner λευκα(ν)θίζω) is intransitive, whereas λευκαίνω is generally (and apparently here) transitive. The poetical intransitive use is not likely to have been part of the commentator's vocabulary.

Fr. 5

```
      ·      ·    ·
   ]  λειφ[
   ]νονγενο[
   ]  ηϲαϲ.[
   ]..’εκατοι.[
5  ]  γαρ.[.]..[
   ]  ενηι[
   ][ ]  [
      ]α.[]..[
      ·      ·    ·
```

Fr. 6

```
       ·      ·    ·
   ]ρεϲκετο[
   ]  [
   ].ιμ[
   ]ντ[
       ·      ·    ·
```

Fr. 5 3 .[, the left-hand end of a cross-stroke level with the overhang of ϲ, but τ not particularly suggested   4].., the upper end, slightly above the top of the letters, of a stroke rising to right, followed by scattered dots   .[, two dots, one over the other, about mid letter   5]., the upper left-hand arc of a circle   7 Whatever ink there was has to all intents and purposes vanished   8 After α the lower part of a stroke rising to right   ]..[, the upper parts of two letters, apparently containing parts of circles

Fr. 7

```
      ·    ·    ·
   ]κα[
   ]  εξ[
   ]  π.[
```

Fr. 8

```
      ·     ·    ·
   ]./αυτο.[
   ].οϲτοτ[
       ·     ·    ·
```

Fr. 8 Very much faded
1]., the upper end of a stroke rising from left   .[, shadows perhaps suiting the top left-hand part of ϲ   2]., a cross-stroke level with the top of the letters; perhaps ϲ likeliest

Fr. 8 1 (ἐϲτιν)

Fr. 9   Fr. 10

Fr. 9 1 The start of a stroke rising to right 2]., two dots one above the other .[, a dot on the line and above to right a short stroke with a projection on its right-hand side

Fr. 10 1 Perhaps *a*, represented by the lower right-hand side of the loop and the extreme lower end of the tail   2]., a dot level with the top of the letters .[, a dot a little below the level of the top of the letters   3].., the tip of an upright, followed by the top of a stroke rising to right; perhaps a single κ possible Of λ only the apex .[, the top of an upright

Fr. 11

(a)

     ]   τηννευρην

        ]..   οξυϊν[

        ]   απουτουτο[]..[.].[ ].δι

        ].οιαποτουαλαλκειψ[

5   ]λκιμον.[].υντ..[

       ]ανδρων.[

       ]αυρουν.[

       ]ξυ   [

(b)

        ]   [

               [

    ]απαλεξιαρη   [

    ].οντω[

Fr. 11 There is no external evidence about the interval between *(a)* and *(b)*   2].., a faint forward-sloping slightly concave stroke, followed by a headless upright with foot hooked strongly to right   3].., the lower part of a forward-sloping stroke, followed by the foot of an upright and two specks on the line; perhaps three letters   ]., a trace a little higher than mid letter   4].., the right-hand part of a cross-stroke touching the top of ο   5.[, a slightly concave upright]., a hook to right level with the top of the letters   ..[, the upper part of a loop or circle, followed by the top of a stroke, turning over sharply to left, a little above the general level   ]., a trace suggesting the top right-hand angle of π   6.[, a slightly forward-sloping upright   7.[, the left-hand end of a cross-stroke against the middle of the right-hand upright of ν

Fr. 11 1 seq. νευρήν implies a bow, ὀξυϊν[- probably a spear, cf. Archil. ap. schol. Hom. *Il.* vi 201.

4 ἀπαλεξιάρη not recorded. ἀλεξιάρη Hes. *Op.* 464, Nicand. *Ther.* 861 (ἀ. ῥάμνου, for which Euphorion, fr. 137 P ἀλεξίκακον . . . ῥάμνον. ἀπαλεξίκακος seems to occur once or twice).

Fr. 12

].ια̣[
]ου̣.[
]χο̣μ[
].[

Fr. 12 1]., apparently the bottom and top of a stroke rising left to right   2 .[, traces compatible with the left-hand side of χ

Fr. 13

][ ][
]cτοτηνι.[
]   [
]   [
]ν[

Fr. 13 1 .[, the foot of a slightly forward-sloping stroke

Fr. 14

].α.[
]θαις..[

Fr. 14 1]., a flat trace on the line   Of α only the loop   .[, the lower part of a forward-sloping stroke descending well below the line 2 ..[, the top of a forward-sloping stroke, followed by a short horizontal stroke level with the top of the letters; possibly to be combined as π

Fr. 15

].[
]θα[
]ιγε[
]κα̣[

Fr. 15 1 The foot of an upright   4 Of α[only the base of the loop

Fr. 16

]   [
] .[
] χ[
]ροια[
] κ[

Fr. 16 1 .[, elements of a forward-sloping stroke, e.g. γ   4 In the left-hand margin a sign in black ink like a slightly tilted z

Fr. 17

].[
2 ll. stripped
] ╱o[
] λ[

2820. EGYPTIAN HISTORY

The following fragment of a roll on its front contains part of a historical work, what survives relating to measures taken, possibly in the second quarter of the first century B.C., by a person of some authority in Egypt. The details are too indefinite or too uncertain to make much of a contribution to knowledge, but incidentally a partial solution is provided of a problem in a quite unrelated text (ll. 11 seqq. note).

The historical text is written in a medium-sized, rather heavy example of a common type of round hand, comparable with **220** and assignable to the first half of the second century. On the back are parts of two columns of which I cannot specify the nature in a hand verging, as well as I can see, towards cursive and perhaps of the third century.

Col. i　　　　　　　　　　　Col. ii

```
        ]    μεταπεμποιτο[            ] [
        ]    αφιϲταϲθαικαιδια            [
        ]    τουτο[. . . .].ϵπλει          [
        ]    ωτων.[. .]νῳν          ] ]υα[
5    ]        [.]χαλκευεκ[. . .].η[      ]  κατ[
     ]    [    .]πατραϲνα.[          ]  κοτ[
        ]    μϵτατονεκε[            ]  πιφ[. .]ϵϲτα[
          ]  θανατονωϲ.[.].           τωνενθ.[.]. . .[
          ]  ϵικοϲεξημϵ.[  ]          ϵπιτουτουϲουπρ.[
10        ]  μενονπαλινεξ            [.]οϲανεπλειπ.[
          ]  ηει.ϵφρουρα[[ι]]ϲϵ [     ]  αλλητη[
             ταιϲ
          ]  πιτηϲχωραϲεμ  [         ] τραϲπα[
        ]    βολαιϲ[.]ϲτηκα[         ]λα.[
          ]  πανταοϲαπρο[
15        ]  πολεμονηνϵ[                 .     .      .
          ]  τρεπιζενωϲτ.[
             ]..α[.]ο.εντειλ[
                ]ολαβω.[
             ].[. . .]περι[
20        ]  βαϲαιγυ[. . .]ουϲτων
          ]  αλλωνειναιμα[
          ]  χιμωτατουϲπρω[
          ]  τονμενπρουτρε[
          ]  πεναυτουϲεκ[
25        ]  ϲιωϲεπιτηνϲτ.[
          ]  . . .ανωϲδουκ.[
          ]  νειχοντοπροϲ[
          ]  ..[]νατ..ϵ. . . .[].[
             ]λϵ.ϵτο[
30          ]ϲο..[
```

Col. i 3]., a cross-stroke as of π or τ; where it touches ϵ there appears to be the start of a stroke curving down concavely to right, perhaps representing a correction　　4 .[, the lower part of an upright, followed by a dot on the line; perhaps two letters　　5]., τ, or possibly π　　6 .[, prima facie the left-hand side of υ, but the ink is obscured by dirt　　11 Between ι and ϵ a dot on the line Above υρα traces of which the middle one resembles ι, but perhaps all offsets　　13 Above the line

Col. i   Col. ii

μεταπέμποιτο [
ἀφίϲταϲθαι καὶ διὰ
τουτο[   ]τε πλεί-   Three lines lost
ω τῶν . [ ]νων   .υα[
5   [ἐ]χάλκευε κ[αὶ].η[κατ[
    .]πατραϲ ναυ[κοτ[ἐ-
    μετὰ τὸν ἐκε[ίν-   πιφ[αν]εϲτα[τ-
    θάνατον ὥϲπ[ε]ρ   των ἐν Θή[β]αιϲ[
    εἰκὸϲ ἐξημελ[η-   ἐπὶ τούτουϲ οὐ πρ.[
10 μένον πάλιν ἐξ-   [.]οϲ ἀνέπλει π.[
    ήει κ⟨αὶ⟩ φρουρὰϲ ἐ-   ἄλληι τη[
    πὶ ʼταῖϲʼ τῆϲ χώραϲ ἐμ-   τραϲ πα[
    βολαῖϲ [ἵ]ϲτη κα[ὶ   λα.[
    πάντα ὅϲα πρὸ[ϲ
15 πόλεμον ἦν ε[ὐ-   .   .   .
    τρέπιζεν ὥϲτε[
    ]..α[.]ο.εντειλ[
        ]ολαβὼν[
    ].[ ]περὶ [Θή-
20 βαϲ Αἰγυ[πτί]ουϲ τῶν
    ἄλλων εἶναι μα-
    χιμωτάτουϲ πρῶ-
    τον μὲν προὔτρε-
    πεν αὐτοὺϲ ἐκ[ου-
25 ϲίωϲ ἐπὶ τὴν ϲτρ[α-
    τείαν ὡϲ δ' οὐκ ἠ[-
    νείχοντο προϲ[
    ..[]νατ..ε....[].[
    λε.ετο[
30]ϲο..[

        .   .   .

the left-hand dot of a *trema*   16 .[, the top left-hand arc of a circle   17].., the top of an
upright, perhaps followed by the top of ϲ, but it would be abnormally long   Of ọ only the top left-
hand side; it is followed by a cross-stroke touching the top of ε   19].[, a flat trace on the line

26 seqq. The left-hand parts blurred   27 Above the second ν what looks like a coarse rough breathing   28 ..[, the tip of a tall upright, followed by the tip of a stroke at the level of the top of the letters   After τ the upper part of two uprights with other ink part or all of which may be casual   After ε perhaps ιβ.ε.[, but here again casual ink and damage to the surface may produce illusion   30 ..[, the top of an upright, followed at an interval by a short nearly horizontal stroke above the level of the top of the letters

Col. ii 9 .[, the top of a stroke level with the top of the letters   10 .[, the left-hand arc of a circle   12 Of ᾳ only a trace of the loop and the top of the right-hand stroke   13 .[, about level with the top of the letters the upper left-hand arc of a small circle, followed by a dot; ω one possibility

Col. i 1 seqq. Perhaps, '⟨intending⟩, if he were summoned, to revolt'. Then, διὰ τοῦτο 'for this reason'.

3 seqq. If χαλκεύειν is here used metaphorically, for κατασκευάζειν or the like, I can adduce no good parallel. χαλκεύεται at Aristoph. *Eq.* 469, though used metaphorically, is one of a group of words referring to handicrafts (τεκταινόμενα, γομφούμενα, κολλώμενα, συμφυσώμενα, συγκροτοῦσι) assembled I suppose to guy Cleon's style.

I can make no plausible suggestion for .[.(.)]νων, but I should guess that τὰ ..]πλείω 'the greater part' of them, not πλείω 'more' than them, was meant.

5 seqq. I should have thought a probable reconstruction of these lines was: κ[αὶ τὸ] τῆ[ς Κλε|ο]-πάτρας ναυ[τικὸν | μετὰ τὸν ἐκε[ίνης | θάνατον ὥσπ[ε]ρ | εἰκὸς ἐξημελ[η|μένον πάλιν ... καὶ φρουράς κτλ. But there are the following objections: the addition of ςκλε at the end of l. 5 makes a line longer than the longest of those surviving; the expected verb, to mean with πάλιν 'rehabilitated' or the like, cannot be got out of εξηει (or εξηει.ε) ;[1] καί is either represented by κε, or, if the verb ends in .ε, is omitted altogether. I cannot meet any of these objections, though it may be worth while to mention the possibility that εξη is a mistaken repetition from the preceding line.

If the text had τὸ τῆς Κλεοπάτρας ναυτικόν, it would, or might, be relevant to note that there were sixty Egyptian ships at the battle of Actium, Plutarch. *Ant.* 64; 66. But there are many Cleopatras besides the daughter of Ptolemy Auletes.

11 seqq. ἐμβολή 'a place where a frontier can be crossed'. This usage, not attested for Herodotus or Thucydides, is found in Xenophon at *Hell.* iv 7, 7 τειχίςαι φρούριόν τι ἐπὶ ταῖς παρὰ Κηλοῦςαν ἐμβολαῖς (cf. ibid. v 4, 48). It must also now be recognized in the fragment of Aeschylus published as **2256 fr. 8**, where ll. 7 seqq. should be rendered: οἱ δὲ γῆς ἐπ' ἐμβολαῖς | ..]μωι λέλυνται, δαΐας πεπαυμέ[νοι | ςάλ]πιγγος, οὐδὲ φρουρί[ω]ν ἐξ...[.].['the frontier guards can go home, war being now over for them'. The problem is only partly solved. I cannot account for the variant or correction -πο- for -βο-, or plausibly complete -μωι. -λας for -λαις (although there is a worm-hole between a and ς, I do not think there is room for an *original* iota) and -λην- for -λυν- seem to be simply mistakes.

14 seqq. I can find no satisfactory parallel for this form of expression, the nearest being Thuc. ii 17 τῶν πρὸς τὸν πόλεμον ἥπτοντο. But I should have expected χρήςιμα, ἐπιτήδεια, or the like, to be made explicit.

19 seqq. I do not know whether the Egyptians of Thebes are elsewhere said to be the most warlike of the Egyptians. According to Thucydides, i 110, the most warlike were the marshmen (of the Delta), μαχιμώτατοί εἰςι τῶν Αἰγυπτίων οἱ ἕλειοι. But it may be observed that Herodotus, ii 164 seqq., says that there were two γένεα of μάχιμοι in Egypt, of which one, the Ἑρμοτύβιες, occupied among other places νῆςος ἡ Προςωπῖτις (in the Delta), the other, the Καλαςίριες, among other the Θηβαῖος νομός.

23 seqq. Since what is meant is plainly 'he urged them to go voluntarily on the expedition' (not 'he gladly urged them on the expedition'), as, apart from general considerations, is implied by 'but when they jibbed', I should have thought that ἰέναι or some such infinitive could not legitimately be omitted.

29 I think λεύετο would be acceptable, but I can recognize no part of εβου at the end of the preceding line.

---

[1] I have contemplated ἐξήκει (for which ἐξηκεῖτο or more generally the simple ἠκεῖτο would be expected) and cannot recommend it.

2821. PEDIGREE

The general nature of these lines seems clear but they present peculiarities that I do not understand, in particular, the absence of the father from the stages of the descent.

The text is written on the front of the piece of which **2802** occupies the back, but it is written across the fibres, that is, as might be expected in a pedigree, from side to side of the height of the roll and from top to bottom of its length.

The hand is a neat little unpretentious bookhand to be dated about the middle of the second century.

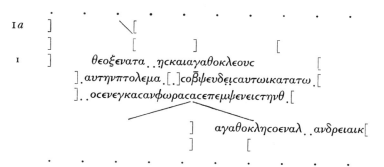

3].., two uprights; πρ not at all suggested, the absence of the loop of ρ being particularly objectionable

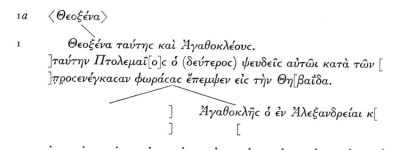

1 seq. The only Theoxena hitherto known to history was the person mentioned in Justin xxiii 2, 6 'Agathocles . . . uxorem suam Theoxenam genitosque ex ea duos parvulos . . . Aegyptum, unde uxorem acceperat, remittit.' This act took place just before Agathocles' death, 289 B.C., the king of Egypt being at that time Ptolemy I. Obviously ταύτης refers to this Theoxena, whose daughter was given her mother's name.[1]

2 'Ptolemy II caught Theoxena jr. bringing to him false ⟨accusations⟩ against the . . . and banished her to the Thebais.' I do not know whether exile to Upper Egypt is a form of punishment recorded elsewhere.

[1] Whether *duos parvulos* must mean two small boys or could mean a small boy and a small girl I must leave to better Latinists to tell me. There is no visible provision in the pedigree as written for any other entry besides Theoxena jr. under l. 1*a*.

4 Agathocles apparently the son of Theoxena jr. and named after his grandfather. The left-hand branch shows that the name of a brother or sister is lost. Why then is there no left-hand branch descending from ⟨Θεοξένα⟩, whom we know from Justin to have had two children?

2822. Hesiod, *Catalogue* ?

It is a reasonable presumption that the two following scraps come from a roll containing the *Catalogue* or a composition not readily distinguished from it, but I have not been able to recognize their contents in the texts of that work (or attributed to it) hitherto published, plentiful as they now are.

The manuscript is in a medium-sized firm upright uncial without lection signs, to be dated, I suppose, in the late first or early second century.

Fr. 1

```
               .      .     .
(a)  ].αβρω.[
(b)  ]α      [
     ]cατακοιτ[
     ]εοιο  [
     ].εχουc.[
               .      .
```

Fr. 1 Ll. *a*, *b* in a clumsy hand in the upper margin may have nothing to do with the verses

(a)]., the lower part of a stroke curving down from left   Of β only the lower half   3]., the tip of an upright   .[, a sloping stroke opposite the overhang of c, presumably representing α, but not particularly suggesting it

Fr. 1 Ll. 1 seqq. Cf. **2490** ll. 17 seqq. (fr. 59 M–W)

Fr. 2

```
          .      .      .
        ]..ρει.[
        ]νοcου[
        ]ητεcτε[
        ]θοcδεκ[
  5     ]ηνκαλλ[
        ]τωνι[
        ]χαιονε.[
        ]ειcε.[
        ]δαιδε.[
 10     ]ευcτη.[
        ].νευc[
        ].ενε.[
          .      .      .
```

Fr. 2 1] . ., off the line a short arc of the lower right-hand side of a circle, followed by the lower part of an upright   . [, the foot of a slightly forward-sloping stroke   7 . [, the upper part of an upright perhaps turning over to right at the top   8 . [, apparently η but very close to the edge   9 . [, γ or the left-hand part of π   10 . [, the extreme left-hand base angle of δ suggested   11] ., the right-hand arc of a circle   12] ., a dot level with the top of the letters   . [, the tip of an upright

Fr. 2 5 This collocation of letters at **2481** fr. 5 (*a*) i 9, **2487** fr. 1 i 14, **2493** l. 1, H l. 56 (frr. 23 (*a*) 15; 129, 14; 229. 1; 204, 94 M–W)

2823. CALLIMACHUS, *Hekale*?

The reason for suggesting that the following scrap may represent a copy of the *Hekale* is to be found in l. 8. The letters αιγεοc are susceptible of several constructions— as parts of more than one word, as αἴγεοc (once in the *Odyssey* for αἴγειοc), and as Αἰγέοc. The last, which appears to me much the likeliest, identifies the piece in which it occurs as verse or, if prose, as Ionic prose. Αἰγέοc is found twice in Herodotus, but these lines are not from Herodotus. In verse I have found it in only one place, Calli- machus fr. 232 ἥ δ' ἐκόηcεν τούνεκεν Αἰγέοc ἔcκεν, which is assigned to the *Hekale*, and this may therefore be assumed, till disproof, to be the source of the passage. The identification is of no immediate value, as I can identify no other verse of the *Hekale* above or below.

The writing runs across the fibres, but the fibres of the other side, which is blank, are also vertical, so that the usual distinction between front and back cannot be made.

The hand is a good specimen of the common rounded type, comparable with e.g. **2161** ascribed to the second century.

```
              .      .      .
           ] . . αδα[
           ]νμαγεπ[
           ]αιηcαπ[
           ]γαcουκ[
     5     ]ηδυνο[
           ] . . αγα . [
           ]εμονα[
           ]αιγεοc[
           ]αξενο . [
    10     ] . ποκα . [
           ] . παλλαδ[
           ] . επρωτ[

              .      .      .
```

1].., the lower end of an upright descending below the line and curling to right, perhaps ρ, followed by a short horizontal stroke off the line, perhaps the base of ϲ   6].., apparently the base of a circle, followed by a cusp on the line (too low for the middle of ω)   ạ broken, but I think likelier than λ   γ headless, but suggested by the spacing   .[, broken, possibly ν   7 ạ[does not account for all the ink; perhaps struck out   9 .[, the top of an upright; ν not suggested   10]., the upper end of a stroke rising from left; the right-hand horn of υ suitable   .[, perhaps a dot level with the top of the letters   11]., perhaps the bottom right-hand angle of ν   12]., the right-hand end of a cross-stroke touching the top of ε

Addendum to **1792**

Another fragment of **1792** (Pindar, *Paeans*), which may be numbered 139, contains syllables which recur in **2442** fr. 32 i 16–19:

.   .   .

]οι[

]ατιϲ[

]απα[

]φιπ[

.   .   .

Though separated from **1792** fr. 31 by no more than five lines it has no great similarity to it.

P. Berol. 21114 is also from **1792**. It was kindly sent me by Dr. H. Maehler, but I did not succeed in discovering any relation between it and the rest.

INDEX TO NEW CLASSICAL TEXTS

(Figures in small raised type refer to fragments, small Roman figures to columns. An asterisk (*) denotes a word in the text about which for various reasons there is room for uncertainty, a small circle (°) a word conjectured in the commentary. References to words from the ancient comments on the papyrus are enclosed in round brackets. Words not to be found in Liddell, Scott, Jones, Greek–English Lexicon, or the supplement to it, are marked with a cross (×). The article is not indexed.)

Ἀγαθοκλῆς 2821 1, 4.
ἀγαθός *2803 6 6.
ἀγλαός 2816 1 2.
ἀγορεύω 2814 29.
ἄγρα 2817 20.
ἀγρώστης 2817 21.
ἀγρώτης (vel -τηρ) °2817 14.
ἄγχι 2814 22.
ἀδάματος °2805 10.
ἀδήριτος 2818 12.
Ἀδρήστεια °2818 4.
ἀ(ι)εί 2813 1 i 14 2815 1(a) 3
  2816 1 10 2817 9.
ἀέριος 2816 1 8.
ἀζαλέος 2817 11.
ἀζομ[2815 5 4.
ἀήρ 2816 1 6.
ἀθλέω 2812 1(a) ii 2.
ἆθλον 2813 1 ii 8.
αἶα 2816 1 14.
Αἰγέος (vel αἴγεος?) 2823 8.
Αἰγίμιος 2815 2(a) 9 (bis).
Αἰγύπτιος 2820 i 20.
αἰδοῖος *2807 1 10.
αἰδώς *2807 1 10.
αἰθήρ 2816 1 14.
αἰπεινός 2818 8.
αἰπολο[2817 14.
αἱρέω *2804 1 9.
αἶσα 2814 30.
Αἴσηπος 2817 17.
αἶσχος 2815 1(b) 8.
αιτια.[2813 12 4.
αἰχμητής *2814 28.
αἶψα 2817 3.
ἀκαλός °2818 11.
ἀκούω 2806 1 i 5 2812 1(a) ii 17.
ἄκρηβος 2804 1 18.
ακρο- *2813 1 i 23.
ἀλαλκεῖν 2819 II 4.
Ἀλεξάνδρεια 2821 4.
ἀλήθεια 2812 1(a) ii 13.

ἄλκιμος 2814 31 *2819 II 5.
Ἀλκμάν 2802 5, 17 2812 1(a) i 7.
ἀλλά 2806 1 i 5 2813 1 ii 31
  2819 1(a) 16, 4 2, 8 (bis).
ἀλλήλων 2816 1 13.
ἄλλος 2806 1 i 10 2820 i 21, ii
  11.
ἄλοχος °2803 3 10.
ἅλς 2812 1(a) ii 34 *2815 1(a) 5.
ἀλύσκω °2815 1(a) 4.
ᾱμα[2815 3(e) 3.
ἅμα *2815 2(a) 18.
ἀμάω 2811 4 4.
Ἀμμώνιος *2811 5(a) 3.
Ἀμύντης °2819 2 1.
ἀμφ[2819 4 3.
ἀμφί 2812 1(a) ii 28.
ἀμφότερος *2815 2(a) 10.
ἄμφω *2815 3(e) 5.
ἄν 2806 1 i 8 2812 1(a) ii 19
  2814 26.
ἀνάγυρος 2813 12 2.
ἀνακρούω 2813 5 15.
ἀναλκείη 2815 1(a) 13.
ἀναπλέω 2820 ii 10.
ἀνάσσω 2815 1(a) 16.
ἄνειμι 2817 20.
ἀνέχω 2820 i 26.
ἀνήρ °2807 1 9 °2813 1 i 14 2815
  1(b) 6, 6 3, *6 *2819 1(a) 15.
ἄνθρωπος 2807 1 2 2813 1 ii 39
  2815 1(a) 6.
ἀντί 2812 1(a) ii 38, 39 2813 9 3.
ἀντίγραφον 2819 2 3.
ἄξιος 2806 1 i 5.
ἀοζέω (ἀοςδέω) 2819 4 4.
ἀοιδή 2816 1 6.
ἄορνος 2819 4 7.
×ἀπαλεξιάρη 2819 II 4.
ἀπαξάπας *2802 20.
ἀπαπαπαῖ 2805 8.
ἅπας 2806 1 ii 8.

ἀπειλέω *2812 1(a) ii 11.
ἀπείριτος 2816 1 14.
ἀπείρων 2816 1 9.
ἄπιος 2801 5.
ἄπλητος 2816 1 15.
ἀπό 2805 10 2813 1 i 38 2819
  II 3, 4.
ἀποδίδωμι °2812 1(a) ii 11.
ἀποκλείω 2810 16.
ἀποκτείνω 2804 1 23.
Ἀπόλλων 2812 1(a) ii 1, *4, 9, 15,
  18, 21.
ἀποπλάσσω *2819 1(a) 7.
ἀπόρνυμαι 2816 1 4.
ἀποσεύομαι 2816 1 5.
ἀποστέλλω 2813 1 i 2.
ἀποστυπάζω 2811 5(a) 6.
ἀππαπαῖ °2809 8 2.
ἅπτω *2818 11.
Ἀργανθώνη *2817 19.
ἀργής 2815 3(e) 13.
ἀργηστής *2815 4 4.
αρη[2802 15.
Ἄρης 2818 11.
Ἀριστόνικος *2803 1 i 4.
Ἀρκάς *2814 22.
ἄρσην 2805 10 2806 1 i 8.
Ἀρχίλοχος 2811 5(a) 5.
ἄρχω °2813 1 i 4, 5 15.
ἀσπίς 2814 6.
ἀστήρ *2815 3(c) 2.
ἀστράγαλος °2815 4 7.
ἀσχεδές °2812 1(a) ii 31.
ἄσχετον 2815 1(b) 5.
Ἀταλάντη 2808 1(b) ii 3.
ἀτεχνῶς 2807 1 11.
Ἄτη 2812 1(a) ii 25.
ἄτρακτος 2817 1.
αὖθι 2816 1 16.
αὐλητής 2813 5 14.
αὖος 2809 9(a) 6.
αυπν[*2815 23 3.

αὐτάρ **2812** ¹⁽ᵃ⁾ ii 33.
αὐτός **2802** 13, 18 **2805** 7 **2806**
ᴵ ii 10 **2811** ² 5, ⁵ 10, 11, 13
2812 ¹⁽ᵃ⁾ ii 7, 11 **2813** ᴵ i 3,
*5, ⁵ 25 **2814** 23 **2815** ³⁽ᵉ⁾ 14
2816 ᴵ 7 **2820** i 24 **2821** 2.
αὐτός **2811** ⁵ 10, 11 *2813 ᴵ i 4.
αὕτως **2819** ⁴ 8.
αὔω **2817** 6.
ἀφαιρέω **2803** ⁵ 4.
ἀφίημι **2812** ¹⁽ᵃ⁾ ii 37, 39.
ἀφίσταμαι **2820** i 2.
ἀφρ[**2817** 13.
ἀφραδία **2812** ¹⁽ᵃ⁾ ii 24.
ἄχθος **2813** ᴵ ii 28 (bis).
Ἀχιλλεύς *2803 ⁵ 3.

βαίνω *2803 ⁶ 4 **2814** 22 **2819**
⁴ 11.
βάραθρον °2808 ¹⁽ᵃ⁾ 1.
βασιλεύς **2814** 18.
βασιλη[**2818** 2.
βιάζω **2813** ᴵ i 5.
×βίδυν **2804** ᴵ 27 (cf. *LSJ* s.v.
βίδην).
βινέω **2806** ᴵ i 10.
]βοος **2813** ᴵ ii 9.
βόσκω **2813** ⁵ 8.
×βοτηράρχης °2812 ¹⁽ᵃ⁾ ii 37.
βου[**2815** ³⁽ᵈ⁾ 4 **2819** ¹⁽ᵈ⁾ 28.
βουλεύω **2813** ᴵ ii 20.
βραχύς **2805** 9.
βρένθειον **2804** ²⁽ᵃ⁾ ii 4.
βρηναι.[**2817** 16.
βρίθω *2814 9.
βωμός **2812** ¹⁽ᵃ⁾ ii 36.

γαῖα **2819** ¹⁽ᵃ⁾ 6.
γαλη[ν- **2819** ⁴ 3.
×γαμηλεύω °2804 ᴵ 6.
γάρ **2806** ᴵ i ⁰5, 6 **2808** ¹⁽ᵇ⁾ ii 1, 3
2810 17 **2812** ¹⁽ᵃ⁾ ii 20 **2816**
ᴵ 13 *2818 3 **2819** ² 11.
γαστήρ **2810** 14.
γε **2807** ᴵ 11, 15 **2813** ⁵ 19.
γέλοιος **2813** ᴵ i 32.
γέλως *2813 ᴵ i 24, 25.
γενειάζω **2806** ᴵ i 11.
γένεσις **2816** ᴵ 2.
γένος **2819** ² 2.
γῆ **2809** ᴵ i 10 **2813** ᴵ ii 28 **2817**
16.
γίγνομαι **2802** 14, *18 **2814** 7,
*28 **2819** ⁴ 4.

γλαυκῶπις °2815 ³⁽ᵉ⁾ 17.
γλυκύς **2804** ᴵ 17.
γλῶττα **2813** ᴵ ii 41.
γομφ[**2809** ᴵᴵ 3.
γονή **2805** 9.
γοῦν **2812** ¹⁽ᵃ⁾ ii 5.
γράφω **2812** ¹⁽ᵃ⁾ ii 23 **2813** ᴵ i
4, 6.
(-)γράφω *2819 ² 1.
γυνή **2806** ᴵ i 6.

δαΐζω **2818** 7.
δαίμων **2816** ᴵ 11.
Δαναός °2803 ᴵᴵ 3.
δέ **2802** 7, 15, 19 **2803** ⁵ 7 **2806**
ᴵ i 9, ii 10, 12 **2812** ¹⁽ᵃ⁾ ii
4, 6, *9, *15, 16, *21, 24, 29,
*31, 32, 39, 47 **2813** ᴵ i °9, 12,
13, 14, 37, ii 30, ⁵ 10 **2814** 26,
27, 31, 32, 33 (bis), 34, 36
2815 ¹⁽ᵃ⁾ 3, 5, ³⁽ᵉ⁾ 12, 14, ⁴ 6
2817 3, 5, *20 **2819** ¹⁽ᵈ⁾ 27,
² 3, 6, ⁴ 6, 16 **2820** i 26.
δείδω **2816** ᴵ 13.
δέκα **2806** ᴵ i 9, 10, 11 *2807 ᴵ 9.
δέρκομαι **2803** ³ 9 **2817** 17, 20.
(δεύτερος) **2802** 5 **2821** 2.
δεύω (= δέω) **2814** 26, 33.
δή **2812** ¹⁽ᵃ⁾ ii 25 **2814** 29
*2815 ³⁽ᵉ⁾ 6.
δηλόω **2819** ⁴ 14.
δη]μηγορε[°2813 ᴵ i 3.
δημός °2815 ³⁽ᵉ⁾ 13.
διά **2812** ¹⁽ᵃ⁾ ii 46 **2813** ᴵ i 19,
ii 19 **2819** ⁴ 14 **2820** i 2.
(δια)]μοιράω °2815 ²⁽ᵃ⁾ 23.
διαπέρθω **2815** ²⁽ᵃ⁾ 14.
διαφέρω **2805** 9.
διδάσκω **2813** ᴵ i 36.
δίδωμι **2811** ⁵⁽ᵇ⁾ 12.
διεργάζομαι **2812** ¹⁽ᵃ⁾ ii 22.
διερός *2815 ³⁽ᶜ⁾ 3.
δικαιων[**2806** ᴵ ii 10.
δίκη **2815** ¹⁽ᵃ⁾ 2, °11, ²⁽ᵃ⁾ 11.
Διονύσιος **2812** ¹⁽ᵃ⁾ ii 5.
δίχα **2814** 23.
δοκέω **2812** ¹⁽ᵃ⁾ ii 19 **2813** ᴵ ii
37.
δόμος °2816 ᴵ 10.
δόρπος °2812 ¹⁽ᵃ⁾ ii 32.
δορυσσόος *2815 ²⁽ᵃ⁾ 6.
δοῦπος **2809** ᴵ i 11.
δράκων **2812** ¹⁽ᵃ⁾ ii 23, 34.
δράω **2809** ᴵ i 7.

Δυμάν **2815** ²⁽ᵃ⁾ 10.
δυσκέλαδος **2817** 4.
δῶρον **2816** ᴵ 2.
δωτίνη **2814** 34.

ἐάν (ἤν) **2815** ²⁽ᵃ⁾ 19.
ἐγγυτ[**2806** ᴵ ii 5.
ἐγώ **2807** ² 3 **2813** ᴵ i 33 *2815
²⁽ᵃ⁾ 3 **2816** ᴵ 7.
ἑέ **2805** 8.
ἔθνος **2819** ² 4.
εἰ **2814** 30.
εἴδομαι *2815 ³⁽ᵇ⁾⁺⁽ᶜ⁾ 2.
εἰκός **2820** i 9.
εἰλίπους **2818** 9.
εἰμί sum **2804** ᴵ 16 **2806** ᴵ i 5, 9,
(10) **2808** ¹⁽ᵇ⁾ ii 1, 3 **2809**
⁹⁽ᵃ⁾ 6 °2811 ⁵⁽ᵃ⁾ 14 **2813** ᴵ i
37, ii 33 **2814** 27 **2815** *¹⁽ᵃ⁾
15, *4 3 **2819** ² 4, 7 **2820** i
15, 21.
εἶμι ibo **2815** ²⁽ᵃ⁾ 19.
].ειμ' **2809** ᴵ i 7.
(-)εἴρω **2815** ³⁽ᵍ⁾ 2.
εἰς (ἐς) *2808 ¹⁽ᵃ⁾ 1 **2809** ³ 2,
⁸ 3 **2816** ᴵ 16 **2821** 3.
εἷς **2809** ᴵ i 11.
εἶτα **2806** ᴵ i 10.
ἐκ **2814** 35 *2815 ¹⁽ᵃ⁾ 5 **2817**
20.
ἕκαστος °2813 ᴵ i 9 **2814** 35.
ἑκατοντάς **2818** 9.
ἐκβάλλω **2812** ¹⁽ᵃ⁾ ii 12.
ἐκεῖνος **2805** 4 **2820** i 7.
ἑκούσιος **2820** i 24.
ἐκτέμνω *2817 7.
ἐλαύνω **2812** ¹⁽ᵃ⁾ ii 31.
ἐλεγχείη **2815** ¹⁽ᵇ⁾ 8.
]ελθεῖν **2807** ᴵ 17.
Ἑλικών **2816** ᴵ 5.
Ἕλλην °2814 17.
ἐμβολή **2820** i 12.
ἐμμελέως **2816** ᴵ 12.
ἐμπίπτω **2808** ¹⁽ᵇ⁾ i 1.
ἐν **2802** 4 **2804** ²⁽ᵃ⁾ ii 8 **2805**
5, 9 (**2806** ᴵ i 10) **2810** 23
2811 ⁵⁽ᵇ⁾ 10 **2812** ¹⁽ᵃ⁾ ii 23,
°38, 46 **2813** ᴵ ii 10, ⁵ 14 **2814**
6, *16 **2815** ¹⁽ᵃ⁾ 5, °17, °¹⁽ᵇ⁾ 3
2816 ᴵ 13 **2819** ⁴ 15 **2820**
ii 8 **2821** 4.
ἐναίρω °2817 9.
ἔνδον **2813** ⁵ 21.
ἐνέπω **2814** 15.

καθίστημι 2819 ⁴ 7.
καί (2803 ¹ i 4, *⁴ 4) 2804 ²(a) ii 13 2805 5 2806 ¹ i 7 (bis), 8, 10, 11, ii 7 2807 ¹ 4, *12, *13 2808 ¹(b) ii 4 2809 ¹ i 5, 9,¹¹ 4 2810 *13, 14, 15, 21, 24 2811 ⁵(a) 5 2812 ¹(a) ii 1, 12, 14, 18, 34 2813 *¹ i 4, ii 22, 23, 31, ⁵ 3, 23 2814 29 2815 ²(a) 9, ²(b) 19, 20, ⁴ 6 2816 ¹ 2, 14, 15, 16 2817 7 2818 4, 8 2819 ⁴ 15 2820 i 2, *5, *11, 13 2821 1.
κακορρέκτης 2812 ¹(a) ii 25.
κακός °2805 11 2813 ⁵ 10, 18.
κακ.[2813 ¹ ii 10.
καλός *2818 11.
Κάλυδναι 2812 ¹(a) ii 35.
καρδία (κραδίη) 2817 5.
καρπός 2811 ⁴ 3.
καρτύνω 2812 ¹(a) ii 28.
καρφαλέος °2815 ²(a) 5.
καρχαλέος °2815 ²(a) 5.
Κάσιος 2818 8.
κατά 2802 14 2805 7 2810 20 2811 ⁵(a) 11 2821 2.
καταπτήςςω 2805 6.
×καταχνύω 2812 ¹(a) ii 32.
κατάχρηςις 2812 ¹(a) ii 38.
κατείβω 2819 ⁴ 16.
κατέπεφνον 2814 30.
κατεςθίω °2806 ² 3.
Κελαδώνη 2815 ⁹ 3.
κελαρύζω 2819 ⁴ *13, 16.
κέλευθος 2815 ²(a) 21.
κεν 2814 29, 36.
κεραός *2818 9.
κέρας °2817 3.
κεφαλή 2810 15 2815 ⁴ 6.
κήρ 2815 ¹(a) 4.
κῆτος 2812 ¹(a) ii 21, 31.
κιθαρωδός 2813 ¹ ii 21.
]κλαςθηναι 2807 ¹ 13.
Κλεοπάτρα °2820 i 5.
κλέος 2814 15.
κλοιόν °2813 ¹ i 38.
κλωγμός 2813 ¹ ii 39.
κολωνή 2812 ¹(a) ii 28.
κομίζω 2804 ¹ 19 2813 ¹ ii 35.
].κοπωι 2809 ¹ i 12.
κόρη 2805 10 2811 ⁵(a) 9 *2815 ³(e) 17 2816 ¹ 1.
Κορίνθιος *2813 ⁵ 24.
Κόρωνος °2815 ²(a) 15.

κόςμος °2815 ¹(b) 4 2816 ¹ 9.
κοῦφος 2813 ¹ ii 31.
κουφότης 2813 ¹ ii 30.
].κρατης 2813 ⁵ 20.
κράτος 2815 ¹(a) 3.
κρήνη 2817 12.
Κρονίδης °2814 32.
κρυο.[*2815 ¹¹ 5.
κρύπτω 2805 7.
κρυφῇι 2805 5.
κτυπ.[2809 ¹¹ 5.
κυδα.[2810 4.
κύκλος 2812 ¹(a) ii 41.
κυκλόω 2817 3.
κυλίνδω *2815 ³(g) 4.
κῦμα 2816 ¹ 15.
κυνέω *2815 ²(a) 8.
κύπελλον 2815 ⁴ 10.
κυρίως 2812 ¹(a) ii 45.
κυςοδακνιάω (or -ία?) 2811 ⁵(a) 10.
×κυςοκνηςιάω (or ία?) 2811 ⁵(a) 13.
κυψέλη 2805 5.
κωμῳδέω 2813 ⁵ 9.
κωμῳδία 2813 ¹ i 4, 35, ii 2, *2 4.

λαγχάνω 2815 ¹(a) 13.
λαγών 2818 8.
λαΐνεος 2812 ¹(a) ii 28.
]λαμβάνω 2809 ¹ i 6 *2813 ¹ ii 2 2820 i 18.
λαμπρός °2810 11.
λανθάνω 2805 7.
Λαοκόων *2812 ¹(a) ii 22, 35.
Λαομέδων 2812 ¹(a) ii *1, 3, 10, 21, 25.
λαός 2812 ¹(a) ii 32 2814 27 *2815 ²(a) 18.
λατύπος 2819 ⁴ 10.
λέγω 2810 22, 24 2811 ² 7 2812 ¹(a) ii 14, 44, 45 2813 ¹ i *34, ⁵ 25 2819 ² 6, 10, 11, ⁴ 10.
λεῖος 2819 ⁴ 8, 12, °13.
λείπω 2812 ¹(a) ii 26.
λελίημαι 2816 ¹ 9.
λευκ[2817 12.
λευκα- 2819 ⁴ 18.
λευκαθέω 2819 ⁴ 19.
λευκαίνω 2819 ⁴ 18.
λευκός *2804 ²(a) ii 9.
ληΐζομαι 2812 ¹(a) ii 27.
λιγυρός °2816 ¹ 6.
λόγος 2811 ² 9 2812 ¹(a) ii 12.

λοιπός 2806 ¹ i 5.
λόφος *2812 ¹(a) ii 24.
Λυδικός 2804 ²(a) ii 4.
]λυφανου 2813 ¹ i 19.

μά 2813 ⁵ 11.
μαινάς 2817 21.
μακρός 2817 6.
μάλα *2815 ¹¹ 15.
Μαραθών °2814 16.
Μασσαγέτης 2817 1.
μάχιμος 2820 i 21.
μέγαρον 2814 35.
μέγας 2804 ¹ 4 2805 11 2806 ¹ ii 7 *2807 ¹ 8 2813 ⁵ 13 2816 ¹ 15.
μέλαθρον (*2803 ⁵ 8).
μέλπω 2816 ¹ 7.
μέμονα °2815 ²(a) 14.
μέν 2802 9 *2804 i 12 2806 ¹ ii 11 2812 ¹(a) ii 3, *8, 20 2813 ¹ i *6, 14, ii 28, 29 2815 ³(e) 4 2816 ¹ 18 *2817 14 2820 i 23.
μένος 2816 ¹ 14.
μέςος 2804 ¹ 21 2805 9.
μετά (2806 ¹ i 10) 2812 ¹(a) ii 6 2813 ⁵ 21 2820 i 7.
μεταπέμπω 2820 i 1.
×μετεκβάλλω 2806 ¹ i 3.
μετοι[2819 ² 12.
μέτοικος °2813 ¹ ii 22.
μετρα[2802 20.
μέτωπον 2810 13.
μή °2809 ⁹(a) 7 2813 ¹ i 6, ii 38 2814 30 2816 ¹ 13 2819 ⁴ 12.
μηδέ 2813 ¹ ii 38.
μηδείς 2813 ¹ *32, 34.
μήν *2807 ¹ 11.
μήτε °2811 ⁴ 3, 4 2812 ¹(a) ii 42.
μήτηρ 2813 ⁵ 13.
μικρός °2802 11.
Μιλτιάδης *2814 16.
μιμνήιςκω 2812 ¹(a) ii 7.
μιν 2814 30.
μιςθός *2812 ¹(a) ii 11.
μῖςος 2812 ¹(a) ii 37.
μολπή 2816 ¹ 7.
μόνον 2814 34.
μόρος 2805 10.
Μοῦςα 2816 ¹ 1.
Μυγδον[2817 19.
μῦθος 2806 ¹ ii 12 2812 ¹(a) ii 27 2815 *²(a) 11, ⁴ 1.

φιλο.[**2810** 7.
φλαῦρος **2813** 5 18.
φλέγω °**2805** 11.
φληναφεία °**2802** 3.
φλόξ **2818** 11.
φλυαρέω °**2813** I ii 38.
φοβέω **2805** 4.
Φοῖβος **2812** I(a) ii 1, 29.
φρήν **2804** I 11   **2806** I ii 9   **2814** 31.
]. φροσύνηι **2819** I(a) 16.
φρουρά **2820** i 11.
Φρύξ **2813** 5 11.
]φυγω °**2809** I i 4.
φῦλον **2819** 4 6.
φωράω **2821** 3.

Χαῖρις *** 2811** 5(b) 6.

χαλινο[**2813** 9 1.
χαλκεύω **2820** i 5.
Χάος **2816** I 16.
Χαρίβοια *** 2812** I(a) ii 34.
χάρις °**2803** 7 9.
χείρ **2804** 2(a) ii 9   **2817** 2.
χέλειον °**2809** I i 5.
]χευατο **2815** 4 11.
χορός (**2810** 25 (*bis*))   **2813** I i 13, 36.
χράομαι °**2813** I ii 24.
χρίω **2804** 2(a) ii 3.
χρόνος °**2802** 14.
χρύσεος **2816** I 3.
χώρα **2820** i 12.
χῶρος **2812** I(a) ii 29.

ψάλλω **2804** I 27.

ψευδής **2821** 2.
ψηρός *** 2817** 15.
ψόφος *** 2809** I i 9.
ψύθιος **2812** I(a) ii 26.

ὦ **2809** I i 7.
ὧδε **2814** 32.
ὤιμοι **2804** I 20.
ὦκα °**2816** I 16   **2819** 4 16.
ὦμος **2815** 4 6.
ὥρα **2807** I 18 (*bis*), 19.
ὡραΐζω **2807** I 17.
ὡς *** 2815** 6 7   **2819** 4 7, 8   **2820** i 26.
ὡσανεί **2812** I(a) ii 44.
ὥσπερ **2820** i 8.
ὥστε **2802** 17   **2810** 16   **2812** I(a) ii 17* **2820** i 16.

PLATE I

fr. 2 (a)

2823

2801

fr. 1

fr. 1

2822

fr. 2

2804

fr. 1

21

25

29

35

36

22

26

37

ZANΘEΙ

27

24

31

32

38

19

20

34

39

30

28

23

33

2815

PLATE II

fr. 2

PLATE III

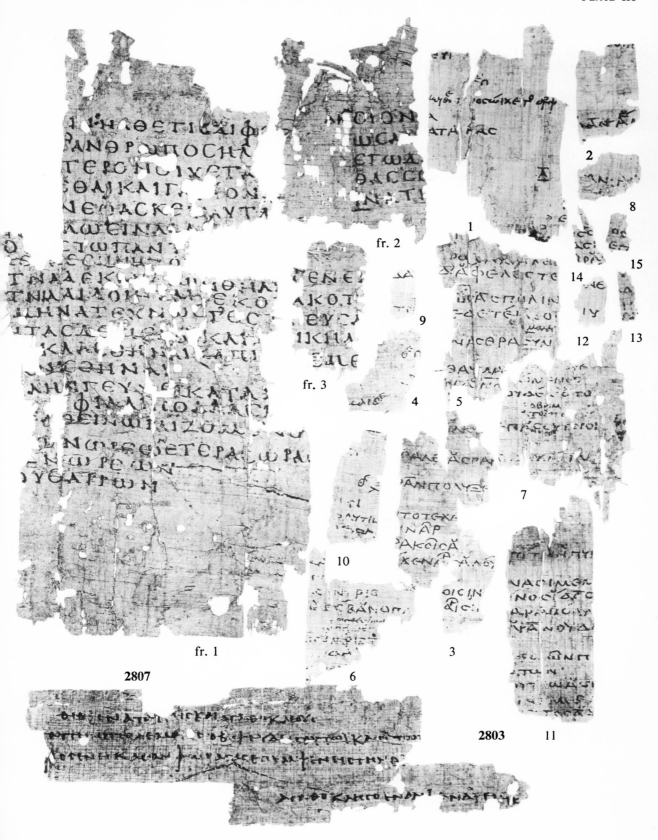

fr. 2

1

2

8

9

14

15

12

13

fr. 3

4

5

7

10

fr. 1

2807

6

3

11

2803

2821

PLATE IV

fr. 1 *(back)*

2803

2814

2810

PLATE V

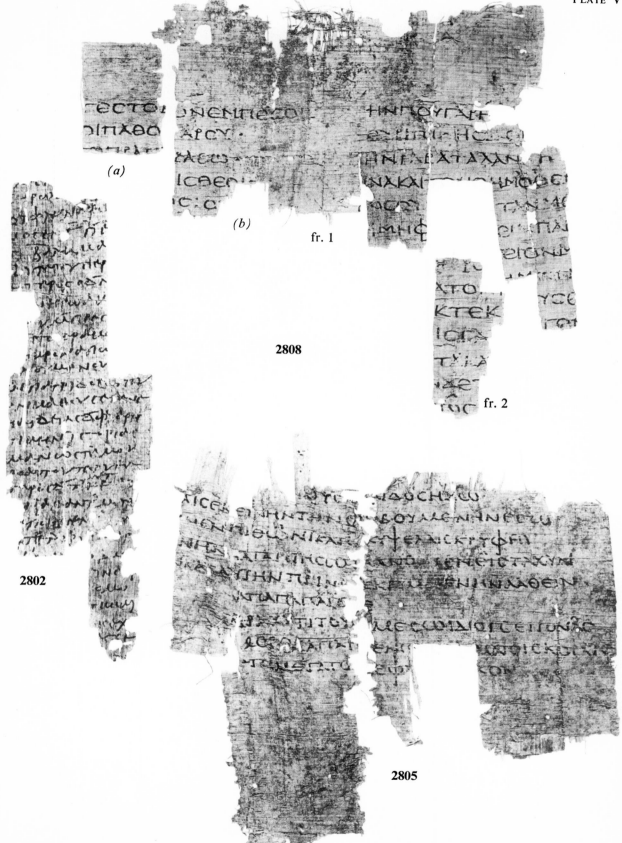

(a)

(b)

fr. 1

2808

fr. 2

2802

2805

PLATE VI

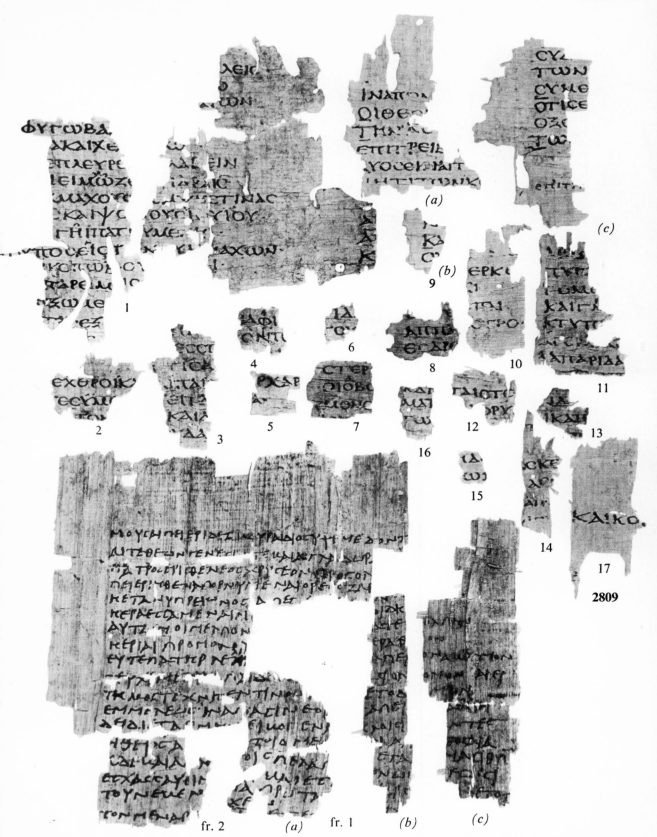

1

2

3

4

5

6

7

8

9

10

11

12

13

14

15

16

17

(a)

(b)

(c)

2809

fr. 2

(a)

fr. 1

(b)

(c)

2816

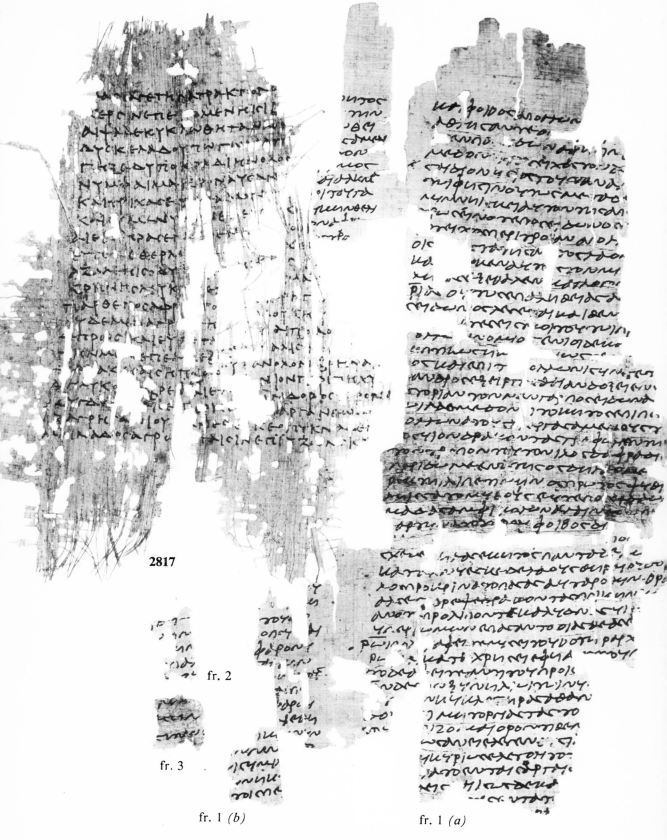

PLATE VII

2817

fr. 2

fr. 3

fr. 1 *(b)*

fr. 1 *(a)*

2812

PLATE VIII

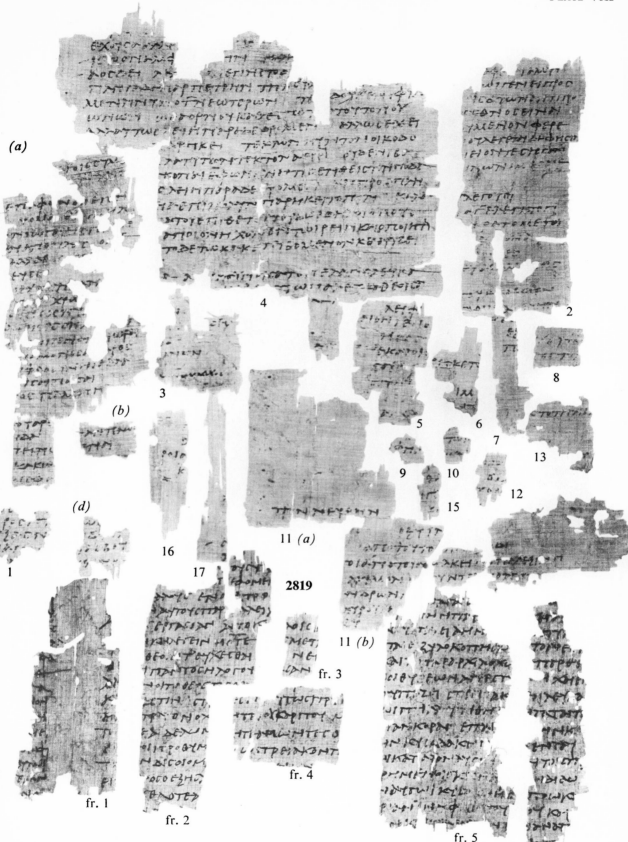

(a)

(b)

(d)

4

2

3

5

6

8

7

13

9

10

12

15

16

11 (a)

1

17

2819

11 (b)

fr. 3

fr. 4

fr. 1

fr. 2

fr. 5

2811

PLATE IX

2820

2818

PLATE X

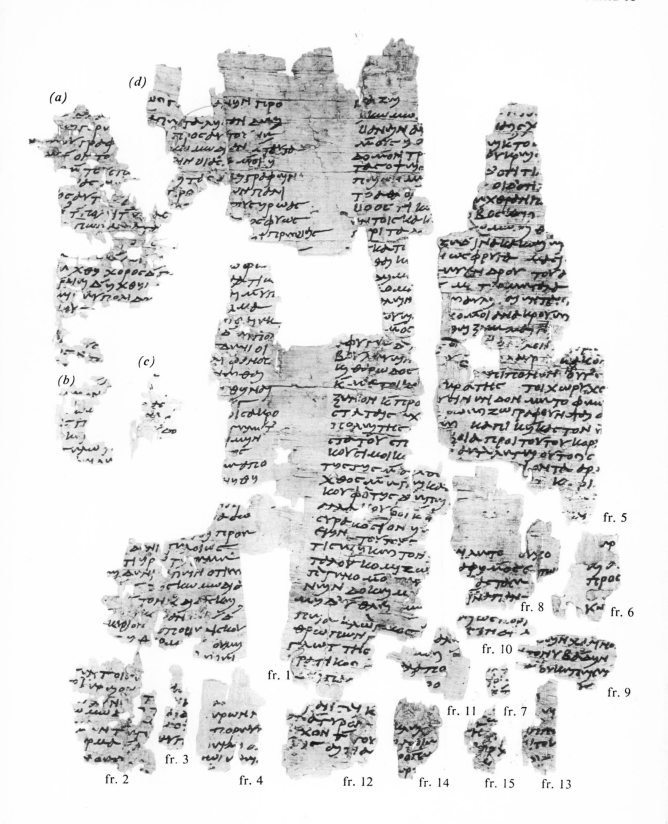

(a)

(b)

(c)

(d)

fr. 5

fr. 8

fr. 6

fr. 10

fr. 1

fr. 9

fr. 11

fr. 7

fr. 3

fr. 2

fr. 4

fr. 12

fr. 14

fr. 15

fr. 13

PLATE XI

(a)

ΞΟΥ·CΙΠΙΟΛΙΑC
ΦΡΟΓΙΝΗΤΕΔΙΚΗΤΕ
ΖΕΥCΕΚΡΑΤΟCΑΙΕΝ
ΝΟΟ·ΛΕΤΟΚΗΡΑCΑΛ
·ΙΑΛΟCΕΝΔΕΘΕΜΙCΤΑ
ICCΟΟΝΑΝΘΡΩΠΟΙC
ΔΙΟCΕΠΙΤΕ·
·ΕΕΙΝ·Χ
ΟΛΕΛ
ΝΚΡΑ
ΙΤΠ··ΡΥΒΡΙΟ··ΙΞΕC
ΙΘΑΜΑΘΩΡΗCΝΠ
ΝΑΛΚΕΙΗΝΤΕΛΕΛΟΓ
ΧΕΦΡΟCΤΝΗΙCΙΝΟ·
·ΕΡΦΙΛΟCΜΑΛΕΟΥC
ΑΛΛΟΙΟΑΝΑCCΩΝ
·ΕΝΙΝΗΙ
·ΤΟΙ
·C·
··Ι·

(b)

(a)
ΙΑΛΛ

(b)
ΤΟ··ΛΟΥCΟ·
ΙΕΛΛΜΡ
ΙΤΑΙ·ΙΑC

(c)
ΔΕΟCC
ΤCΗΔΕΤ
·CΔΕΡΙ
·CΕΠ
ΕΙΝΑΡΗ *(h)*
·ΝΙCΑ·   ·Ν
·ΑΤ·

(d)
·ΙΕ
·ΡΑΤΕ
·ΑΛΛΑΤΙΟC
ΗΝΤΕΘΟΥ
·ΘΓ·

(e)
·Ω
·ΔΕΦΛΕΑΤΙΔΕΚ
ΚΟΥΙΕΝΑΛΛ
ΝΙ·ΗΝΜΕΝΗ
ΑϤΝΑΔΙΤΕ
·ΕΔΗΠΑ
ΗΛ
ΕΝ·
ΘΑ·
·ΚΑΙΤΕ
·ΔΘΕΟΙC·Τ
·····ΠΟΛ
·CΥΠΗΕΙ
ΤΕΩΝΔΕΤΛΝ
ΙΧΘΥΕCΑΓΓΕΤΑ
ΑΥΤCΕΔΕΤΡΟΜΕCΩΝΑ
ΝΗCΩΗΙCΙΠΤΟΙCΙΝΕ
·Θ··ΤΟΙCΙΝΕ
·ΟΡΑ·   ΡΗΝΛΗ
ΟΥΡΗΙΓΑ
ΟΝΙΤΙCΙ·
·ΙC·ΔΙΑΠ
ΑΙΝΘΙΑΟ

(j)
·Ν
ΤΕ·ΥΠ

(f)
ΙΑΝC
ΕΝΔ·
ΚΟΝΙ

(b) *(fr. 1)*
·CΟΙΕΝΤΙΤΙ
·CΤΕΡΗΙΞΝΙ·
·ΑΛΛΙΓ·ΕΡΙΝΕΤΑΙΗΕΠΙΧ
ΙCΗΙΛCΧΕΤΕΝΟΙΝΟΒ
·ΙΡΑCΕΥΑΝ·ΡΑCΙΝ···
·ΤΛΜΕΝ··ΜΟΝΕΠΡΗ
·ΝΕΧΟCΕ·   ·ΕΙΗΤΕC·ΧΟΙC

(g)
·ΜΟΡΑ
ΝΕΕΡΜΕ
·ΤCΑΛΟC
ΥΛΝΔΕΤ
·ΑΧΡΗCΟΥC

fr. 1   fr. 3

2815

PLATE XII

(a)

(b)

(c)

fr. 9

fr. 7

fr. 10

fr. 11

fr. 13

fr. 14

fr. 16

fr. 15

fr. 17

fr. 6

fr. 2

fr. 18

fr. 8

fr. 5

fr. 12

fr. 4

2007. 04. 23   (9.95)